# POLICE DISCRETION

By

KENNETH CULP DAVIS
John P. Wilson Professor of Law
University of Chicago

ST. PAUL, MINN.
WEST PUBLISHING CO.
1975

COPYRIGHT © 1975
By
WEST PUBLISHING CO.
All rights reserved

*Library of Congress Catalog Card Number*: 75–15385

Davis Police Discretion MTB
1st Reprint—1977

# PREFACE

This is a study of police discretion in selective enforcement. The purpose is to try to find or invent better ways to control police discretion in determining whether and when to enforce particular law. The study is based on the practices of the Chicago police, but the analysis may be broadly applicable to other police.

The main facts about selective enforcement in the Chicago police department are clear and simple: The central fact is that the police falsely pretend to enforce all criminal law; the reason for the pretense is that they believe the law requires them to enforce all criminal law but they are unable to. The false pretense is pervasive and has many consequences. Written instructions from top officers (general orders, special orders, and training bulletins) provide for full enforcement, with slight exceptions. But all officers readily acknowledge that some law is never enforced and that some is only sometimes enforced. The false pretense prevents *open* selective enforcement, prevents top officers from making and announcing enforcement policy, prevents special studies of enforcement policy, prevents the use of professional

## PREFACE

staffs for making enforcement policy, prevents enlistment of public participation in policymaking, and discourages efforts of the police to coordinate their enforcement policy with the policy of prosecutors and judges.

The facts stated in the preceding paragraph are quite clear. They are based on 300 interviews with Chicago police at all levels. Each of the top six officers has separately confirmed those facts to me. None volunteered them in the form I have stated them, but each of the six acquiesced in my leading questions. Each resisted some of my ideas; none resisted my statement of the main facts.

The analysis of the problem of what to do on that factual foundation is what matters, and the cornerstone of the analysis is in chapter 4, which reaches the somewhat surprising conclusion that *open selective enforcement is legal*. The widespread—perhaps universal—assumption of American police has long been that the police through an enforcement policy may not legally make noncriminal what a legislative body has made criminal. Even when that assumption is supported by legislation explicitly requiring full enforcement of all criminal law, I believe it cannot prevail, because of a combination of reasons that seems to me enough to override full enforcement legislation—(1) the frequent legislative intent with respect to specific criminal stat-

## PREFACE

utes that enforcement officers should cut them back, (2) the usual appropriation of only enough for something like half to two-thirds of full enforcement, and (3) other reasons stated in chapter 4 that are too elaborate for quick statement.

The proposition that open selective enforcement is legal is the foundation for the rest of my thesis. The thesis is (1) that the false pretense should be terminated, (2) that the selective enforcement policies should be open, (3) that top officers should make the overall policies, (4) that they should use professional staffs for making it, (5) that for much of it they should use rulemaking procedure of the kind that federal administrative agencies customarily use, and (6) that patrolmen should no longer make overall enforcement policy.

The part of the thesis pertaining to rulemaking is further developed in chapters 5, 6, and 7, because misconceptions about rulemaking are prevalent. Fourteen separate reasons for open rulemaking on selective enforcement are summarized at the end of chapter 5; each seems convincing and the combination of all fourteen seems overwhelming. Chapter 6 explores fascinating potentialities of judicially required police rulemaking, now in its beginning stages. The Supreme Court of the United States has been spending an inordinate portion of its time fashioning the details of

## PREFACE

the exclusionary rule, aimed at only two or three percent of police activity; police rulemaking, required and reviewed by courts, will consume less judicial time and has promise for bringing nearly all police activity under legal control, including selective enforcement. The final chapter searches for the right mix of rule and discretion, rebuts the common misunderstanding that rules necessarily replace discretion, emphasizes the utility of rules to reinforce and to guide discretion, and proposes that patrolmen should have discretion to individualize the application of enforcement policy that is centrally made.

My basic approach is to try to apply to the police the thinking about administrative law, in which I have specialized for thirty-five years, and especially to transfer some of the know-how that has developed around our most advanced administrative agencies to the police, who seem to me not at all advanced. My effort to apply to the police the basic ideas of my book on Discretionary Justice— A Preliminary Inquiry (1969) seems to me to have yielded some refinement of those ideas. My belief in the potentiality of police rulemaking is stronger than ever, and I am gratified that that movement has gained a good deal of momentum during the past six years. On one question I have reversed my position; my former view that planned non-

## PREFACE

enforcement of some criminal law is illegal now seems to me unsound, even though almost everyone agrees with it. The legal analysis in chapter 4 penetrates the problem much more deeply and compels the opposite answer, I think. What has changed my position is not more facts, but what I deem to be better understanding.

That this study is founded on facts about the Chicago police does not mean that the analysis is inapplicable to the police of other American cities. Because selective enforcement seems to spring up whenever criminal legislation overshoots, and because all states have had legislation which enforcement officers have had to cut back, pretended full enforcement might be found everywhere or almost everywhere. Yet I have no specific information as to how prevalent it is; the literature on selective enforcement is too fragmentary to extract general conclusions from it.

The interviewing for this study started at the center of the stage and gradually moved to the edge of the stage and then partly off the stage. The results of the interviewing were less than completely satisfactory. Yet the main facts on which the analysis in this study rests seem to me entirely clear. The manner in which the facts were gathered is worth reporting, even if it is not of prime

## PREFACE

importance. An account of the interviewing is set forth in the appendix.

**Acknowledgments.** My five research assistants turned out to be exceptionally able and diligent. Their work has been not merely good but excellent, and I am especially grateful to them. Four of them were between the second and third years of study at the University of Chicago Law School: James Miller, David Morgans, Henry Ordower, and Robert Weber. Bruce Washburn had just graduated from the University of Iowa Law School, where he had participated in a law review project involving interviewing police in three Iowa towns, 68 Iowa L.Rev. 893 (1973).

All of us are grateful to the 300 police who allowed us to interview them.

Valuable suggestions, which I much appreciate, have been made by six friends who read the manuscript—Professor Walter Gellhorn of Columbia University, Professor Herman Goldstein of the University of Wisconsin, Professor Yale Kamisar of the University of Michigan, Judge Carl McGowan of the Court of Appeals for the District of Columbia, Dean Norval Morris of the University of Chicago, and Professor Frank Remington of the University of Wisconsin.

K. C. D.

Chicago, Illinois
June, 1975

# TABLE OF CONTENTS

|  | Page |
|---|---|
| PREFACE | III |

**Chapter**
1. **Examples of Police Enforcement Policy** ... 1
   - Do the police enforce all criminal law? ... 1
   - Twenty quick samples of nonenforcement of criminal statutes and ordinances ... 3
   - Lack of a complainant ... 7
   - Drinking in the park ... 12
   - Disorderly conduct ... 14
   - Purposeful harassment ... 16
   - Prostitution ... 20
   - Informers ... 28

2. **How the Police Make Enforcement Policy** ... 32
   - Research and development ... 32
   - The ingredients of enforcement policy ... 33
   - The role of patrolmen in making policy ... 38
   - Professional staffs and special studies ... 41
   - Procedure ... 46

*TABLE OF CONTENTS*

Chapter

2. **How the Police Make Enforcement Policy**—Continued — Page
   Coordination with other organs of government ............ 48
   Summary ............ 50

3. **The Pervasive False Pretense of Full Enforcement** ............ 52
   The overall picture ............ 52
   The full enforcement legislation .. 54
   Formal administrative action supporting the full enforcement legislation ............ 58
   The police accomplishment ...... 62
   Three possible courses of action for the police ............ 66
   Reasons for getting rid of the false pretense ............ 70

4. **The Legality of Open Selective Enforcement** ............ 79
   The full enforcement legislation is clear on its face ............ 79
   Legislative intent expressed outside the full enforcement legislation, combined with impossibility of full enforcement ..... 80
   Four main types of enforcement problems and the case for legality of selective enforcement 82
   The story of Patrolman X ...... 88

*TABLE OF CONTENTS*

**Chapter**
**4. The Legality of Open Selective Enforcement**—Continued    **Page**
    May a police rule legally provide for nonenforcement of a criminal statute or ordinance? ..... 90
    Some conclusions ............... 95

**5. Rules and Rulemaking Procedure** .. 98
    The need for rules ............. 98
    The movement toward police rulemaking ...................... 99
    Rulemaking procedure .......... 103
    Police authority to make rules ... 107
    Reasons for rulemaking on selective enforcement .............. 112

**6. Should Courts Require Police Rulemaking?** .................... 121
    Some recent administrative law .. 121
    The extra-judicial positions of Judges McGowan and Wright .. 125
    Cases requiring police rulemaking 129
    Legal approaches to judicially required rulemaking ............ 131

**7. The Right Mix of Rule and Discretion** ........................ 139
    The present mix ................ 139
    Should police discretion be eliminated? ....................... 140

## TABLE OF CONTENTS

**Chapter**

7. **The Right Mix of Rule and Discretion**—Continued  **Page**

    Why unnecessary discretion is undesirable ........................... 143

    Why confining, structuring, and checking of necessary discretion is desirable .............. 145

    Rules do not necessarily replace discretion ........................... 149

    Choosing the mix of rule and discretion ............................. 151

    General policy calls for rules; individualizing calls for discretion 158

8. **Summary and Conclusions** ........ 164

APPENDIX ............................... 173

†

XII

# POLICE DISCRETION

## CHAPTER 1

## EXAMPLES OF POLICE ENFORCEMENT POLICY

**Do the police enforce all criminal law?**

The police make policy about what law to enforce, how much to enforce it, against whom, and on what occasions. Some law is always or almost always enforced, some is never or almost never enforced, and some is sometimes enforced and sometimes not. Police policy about selective enforcement is elaborate and complex.

Yet the Chicago police at all levels usually say that their only enforcement policy is to enforce all statutes and all ordinances. They generally say they do not make policy, but when they are pressed they concede they do have some unwritten and often consistent practices about enforcing and not enforcing. When their habits about enforcement or lack of it are predictable, I think they have a

## Ch. 1  ENFORCEMENT POLICY

"policy," even if it is unwritten and even if they deny that they have a policy.

Enforcement policy is unplanned. Top officers generally do not make it, except that occasionally they decide that something should be enforced or should be more vigorously enforced. Top officers do not direct staffs to make studies of what the enforcement policy should be. They hardly ever have meetings for group discussions of such policy. They never assign special problems to professional workers with special training. Most enforcement policy is resolved by drift. Because top officers neglect to do anything about it, those at the bottom of the organization of 13,400 Chicago policemen have to decide what to do whenever they are confronted with a problem. Enforcement policy is made mainly by patrolmen, who are least qualified to make it, and they make it without the benefit of special studies by qualified staffs.

When we have interviewed officers, high and low, to find the reasons for enforcement policy, we have almost always been told something like this: "We don't make enforcement policy. We enforce all law. That's our obligation." When we have asked why an officer enforces something, the answer is that he has to. When we ask why an officer does not enforce something, the answer is: "We can't enforce everything." Those are the two fundamentals, according to what we are told. Rarely does any officer, high or low, try to put the two answers together.

On that background, the first step in this essay about the enforcement policy of the Chicago police has to be to establish the fact that the police do make enforcement policy. Some of the policies are difficult, complex, and variable, as I shall shortly show. But first let us consider some simple and easy samples of nonenforcement.

### Twenty quick samples of nonenforcement of criminal statutes and ordinances.

Although the Chicago police pretend to enforce everything and often seem to fool themselves into believing that they do, they plainly do not. Here are some samples:

1. A 19-year-old standing in a street fired three shots at a woman standing in a doorway of her home but missed. The police apprehended him and knew that neighbors witnessed the shooting. But they released him when the woman asked them to. They explained that they do not ordinarily arrest when a victim is able to sign a complaint but does not do so.

Ch. 1   *ENFORCEMENT POLICY*

2. We asked more than a hundred officers at various levels what they would do in the preceding case, and about two-thirds of them said they would release. One patrolman volunteered that he had witnessed an armed robbery but that he released the robber because the victim so requested.

3. Even when a police officer witnesses shoplifting, the uniform policy is to release the shoplifter if the merchant so requests.

4. Patrolmen often require a juvenile to make restitution for vandalism or a minor theft, but they usually release the juvenile when the owner is satisfied.

5. A patrolman who finds a juvenile drinking something alcoholic is likely to pour out the beverage but is unlikely to take the juvenile into custody.

6. An ordinance makes it a crime to smoke in an elevator, but I have often ridden in an elevator in the police headquarters building with smokers and police and I have never witnessed a gesture toward enforcement.

7. A man who patronizes a prostitute is guilty of a crime under an Illinois statute, and he is also guilty under the more easily enforced ordinance about loitering for purposes of prostitution, but even when the evi-

*ENFORCEMENT POLICY*   Ch. 1

dence is clear and even when officers arrest the woman who is with the man, the officers never arrest the man unless he gives the officers a hard time. In most such cases, the police policy probably cannot be explained in terms of limited police resources.

8. Anyone twelve years old or more who rides a bicycle on the sidewalk is guilty of crime but is almost never given a ticket. Although traffic laws are generally applicable to bicycle riders, the policy is usually one of nonenforcement except in unusual circumstances.

9. An ordinance makes it a crime to drink an alcoholic beverage in the park, but those who telephone the police anonymously to ask whether they may have drinks on a family picnic are usually told that they may. Not only do the police not enforce in absence of disturbance to others, but they acknowledge their nonenforcement to an anonymous caller.

10. Social gambling is openly permitted, even when violation of the Illinois statute is clear. Some officers will stop the gambling when a complaint is made but some will not. None will arrest in absence of either a complaint or a commercial element, except in rare cases when the stakes are extraordinarily high.

Ch. 1   *ENFORCEMENT POLICY*

11.  Many officers say they never arrest for attempted bribery, even if witnesses see the attempt and are willing to testify. Some officers believe that a conviction is too improbable; others say the law is too harsh, given the expectations citizens have developed on the basis of past police practices.

12.  Patterns of systematically permitting parking in no-parking areas are very common.

13.  Almost all motorists know that the police are often lenient about some types of traffic violations.

14.  The Chicago police found that jaywalking does not cause accidents and announced that nothing will be done to enforce the ordinance against jaywalking, but the ordinance remains on the books.

15.  Spitting on the sidewalk is punishable by a fine of not less than $1 or more than $5, but officers unanimously say they do not enforce the ordinance.

16.  Officers who find a couple having intercourse in a parked car generally do not arrest even though the fornication statute has been recently reenacted.

17.  More than nine out of ten patrolmen refuse to arrest for smoking marijuana in public even though the possession of even a

*ENFORCEMENT POLICY*　　Ch. 1

tiny quantity of marijuana is a crime. Supervising officers have generally asserted in our interviews that the arrest should be made, but they generally acknowledge that they do not require their subordinates to comply with their views.

18. All patrolmen refrain from full enforcement of curfew laws, but the variations in nonarrest patterns from one officer to another are wide; some are fairly strict and some are quite liberal.

19. Possession of unlabeled pills is a crime, but most officers say they do not arrest for a small number. Each officer follows his own idea of what the minimum should be for an arrest, with no guidance from superiors.

20. Even one caught in the act of burglary may be released by some officers if the burglar is an informer about narcotics dealers. The more usual reward to an informer is nonprosecution instead of nonarrest. No statute or ordinance authorizes special deals between police and informers, but such deals are a mainstay of enforcement of the narcotics laws.

**Lack of a complainant.**

One vital problem of policy that often has to be answered with respect to both felonies

## Ch. 1  ENFORCEMENT POLICY

and misdemeanors is whether or not an arrest should be made when the victim of a crime is able to sign a complaint but declines to do so. The top officers of the Chicago police department have not answered the question in their formal directives—the "general orders," "special orders," and "training bulletins." The question is answered mainly by patrolmen, who sometimes have and sometimes lack guidance from their supervisors, such as sergeants, lieutenants, watch commanders, and district commanders. The first four items in the list of twenty in the preceding section deal with this problem, but those items call for elaboration.

The case of the 19-year-old who fired three shots at the woman but was released because the woman did not want to sign a complaint is a real case. One of my research assistants was riding in a patrol car with two officers when the call from the woman came in, and the car was one of three cars to respond, with a total of seven officers. Even though the officers knew that witnesses had seen the shooting, they released the boy. I was so startled by my assistant's impression that the seven officers all agreed with the release of the boy that I suggested we make the case the subject of a question to put to a large number of officers in our interviews. What we first found was that patrolmen were almost unanimous that the boy was properly released. Then we found that sergeants and lieutenants were about two to one in favor of release, and that watch commanders and district commanders about equally divided. Of the six top officers of the department, the superintendent and the five deputy superintendents, the answers were four to two *against* the release, and two of the four expressed themselves very emphatically against release.

Most of the patrolmen had rather simple answers, with little reasoning. One said: "When there's no complainant, there's no crime." He further explained that his remark is limited to cases in which victims are able to sign complaints and do not do so. One said: "If the victim doesn't care, why should I?" That view was expressed by a good many. Perhaps the most common answer was: "You can't get a conviction unless the victim voluntarily testifies." When we asked whether witnesses other than the victim would not suffice for a conviction, the usual answer was no. The patrolmen seemed not at all convincing in their view of the legal process, but they seemed to have a rule of thumb that the offender must be re-

Ch. 1   *ENFORCEMENT POLICY*

leased, even for a serious crime, if the victim is able to sign a complaint but refuses.

One sergeant said that in his career he must have been involved in a hundred cases in which a person was shot or stabbed seriously enough to go to the hospital but in which no arrest was made because the victim would not sign a complaint. He said the main reason for his policy is that he wants to protect the victim against retaliation, and he said that his watch commanders have generally agreed with him.

Our interviews show, in general, that the higher the rank of the officer the more likely that he himself will sign the complaint. Several watch commanders and district commanders said quite heatedly that the purpose of the police is to protect the public, not just to satisfy the victim, and that the failure to make the arrest in the case of the three shots was obviously and clearly unsound. But two deputy superintendents quite callously said that the failure is not that of the police but that of the prosecutors. They seemed not at all impressed when I urged each one to consider the probable effect of testimony by the witnesses.

Two assistants in the state's attorney's office expressed the opinion that if the witnesses would give clear testimony, they could win the case. They also said they might subpena the victim. But one assistant supported the police policy of nonarrest, on the ground that conviction was unlikely without the victim's testimony.

One patrolman who agreed with the release explained: "Why, I had the experience of standing in a dark doorway and witnessing a holdup. I stepped out and apprehended the robber. But the victim asked me to let him go, and of course I had to. We never arrest when the victim asks us not to." In answer to a further question, he said it didn't matter that he could himself give testimony as a witness.

To the question whether a shoplifter whose theft is witnessed by an officer should be arrested if the owner or manager prefers not to sign a complaint, the answer was uniformly no. And youth officers were nearly unanimous in saying that they release a juvenile when the owner of stolen or damaged property is satisfied by restitution.

Several facts that come out of our interviews on this subject seem rather vital: (1) The department has no uniform policy. (2) The dominant view of patrolmen is the opposite of the dominant view of the top six officers. (3) The policy is made by the patrolmen, not by the top officers. (4) The supervising officers, such as sergeants, lieutenants, watch commanders, and district commanders, do not require patrolmen to follow their ideas of policy. (5) Patrolmen are trying to appraise the results of legal processes, about which they know little and about which they have misimpressions. (6) Even two of the deputy superintendents had opinions about legal processes that differed from those of two assistants to the state's attorney. (7) Even if patrolmen realize that they need legal advice on such a question, the department has no legal advisers; the theory that the city's corporation counsel gives advice to the police has no reality for patrolmen or other subordinates. The use of assistant state's attorneys is limited to preparing felony cases.

## Drinking in the park.

We telephoned anonymously each of the 21 police districts in Chicago to ask whether we will be arrested if we drink beer on a family picnic in a park. All but 3 gave some sort of answer, but the 3 were noncommittal; 3 said we would be arrested, 4 said we probably would, and 11 said we would not or probably would not be arrested.

In the 1st district, the answer to whether we would be arrested was: "Yes, absolutely," and the answers were about as unequivocal in the 12th, 13th, and 17th districts. But negative answers were unequivocal in the 2d, 3d, 4th, 5th, 14th, 16th, and 19th districts. In the 14th, our question was met with a question: "What do you mean, will we arrest? Look how many people drink in the park. We can't arrest them."

Two facts are noteworthy about the answers—the willingness of 11 of the 21 districts to tell an anonymous caller that he will probably not be arrested for a clear violation of the ordinance if he is quiet and does not disturb others, and the lack of uniformity in the answers from one district to another.

When we interviewed patrolmen on the same question, the nearly unanimous answers were that one will not be arrested for drinking in the park in absence of disturbance to others. But the supervising officers were often uninformed of that policy of patrolmen, and they were often stricter. A good many of them said that for a clear violation an arrest must be made. Lack of arrest, in their view, is a failure of the patrolman to do his duty.

Ch. 1  *ENFORCEMENT POLICY*

In some circumstances, an arrest would be unthinkable. On a summer evening, several hundred Puerto Ricans may gather in Humboldt Park to eat, drink, and be merry. Several officers are there to keep the peace. Arresting for drinking in the park would be out of the question. It would do no good, and it would be likely to cause a riot. Similarly, half the crowd at a rock concert in a park may be drinking and ten or fifteen percent may be smoking marijuana, but the police who are there customarily make no arrest for such offenses. If they were to try to do so, they would have to bring in a large number of officers, and that would serve no good purpose.

**Disorderly conduct.**

Three factual patterns need to be distinguished: (1) The officer who arrests for disorderly conduct believes he has probable cause and he later appears in court to give testimony. (2) The arresting officer thinks he has probable cause but does not appear in court. (3) The arresting officer knows he has no probable cause and has no intent to appear in court; he is using arrest as a sanction.

Of the three, the third is numerically many times as important as the first two in combination. Arrest for disorderly conduct usually is not synonymous with "invoking the criminal process" but is synonymous with imposing punishment—that of being detained, having to go to the station, having to put up bail or to stay in jail, and having to appear in court or forfeit the bail money. Most arrests for disorderly conduct involve an abuse of power by the arresting officer, as most of the officers we have interviewed readily acknowledge. Some of them even take the initiative to boast about how effectively they use the disorderly conduct statute.

The Supreme Court of the United States in a line of unanimous decisions has held that words alone may not constitutionally be an offense unless they are fighting words, but the effective law in Chicago often is that verbal defiance of an officer, without fighting words, is usually punished by an arrest. The police make the effective law on such a subject; the Supreme Court's version of the law is merely some words in a book.

The policy of the department does not stem from top officers, but it is reasonably clear and reasonably uniform: An officer, without disapproval by his superiors, may use arrest as a sanction whenever his emotions impel him to, even though he knows that he has no evidence that any court would accept as tending to prove disorderly conduct, and even though the officer never intends to appear in court to testify against the arrested person. One officer said to us that he has made many arrests for disorderly conduct during the past two years but has not appeared in court on such charges even once.

Arrest for disorderly conduct is a principal weapon in the deliberate harassment of individuals, as shown in the next section.

**Purposeful harassment.**

The police often make their own law and enforce it. Police-made law, with no statutory foundation, is a rather important phenomenon.

One officer proudly told us in an interview that he "knows" that X is a big narcotics dealer, so that whenever X comes out on the street the officer searches him and often finds some excuse to arrest him. When we asked the officer why he does not arrest X for selling narcotics, he said his evidence is convincing but would not stand up in court. When we asked whether he searches without a warrant and without probable cause, he said: "Yes, of course." "Isn't that unconstitutional?" "Perhaps, but it doesn't matter, because we're not trying to get evidence for a court proceeding. You see, the Constitution applies only to getting evidence that will be admitted in court." X is always prepared for the search, the officer says; he never carries drugs or anything related to drugs. So the officer often arrests him. He gave X a ticket when X doubled parked to get a newspaper from a coin machine near the curb; he does not ordinarily give a ticket for that, but making the most of a technical violation is one way of harassing X. Sometimes the officer arrests X for disorderly conduct, even when X is guilty of nothing. The officer says he goes through a ritual to keep such an arrest "honest." He says "move on" and then in the same breath says: "You didn't move fast enough and I'm arresting you for disorderly conduct." The officer chuckles that X has to put up bail money and then appear in court to get it back. He knows that X has no practical remedy against such a false arrest.

Another officer "knows" that Y is a pimp but has no evidence to prove it. When asked how he knows, he said Y lives in a building where other pimps live and that he has seen Y talking with prostitutes. He was displeased when asked whether some non-pimps also live in the building and whether

Ch. 1    *ENFORCEMENT POLICY*

he has seen some non-pimps talk with prostitutes. But he is proud of the fact, which he freely volunteered, that he put sugar in Y's gasoline tank. He thinks that if he can harass Y enough, he can get him out of the district. Reports of this type from patrolmen are very common, but we have found that supervising officers always say they disapprove such practices.

The level of understanding of some officers has been somewhat surprising to us. According to a good many officers we have interviewed—and a good many do express this same view, rather noticeably with about the same vocabulary—all society is divided into two classes of people, the "kinky" (criminal) class and the law-abiding class. The officers can tell which are which by physical characteristics and appearance—mostly hair and dress, but also the look in the eyes. The working principle is that searches of "kinky" people for drugs and handguns are necessary and proper, whether or not the searches would be constitutional if evidence so obtained were presented in court. The drugs and handguns can be seized and confiscated and no question will come to court, they say. The patrolmen say they have no instructions to make such searches but they also say they are not in-

[18]

structed not to. Supervising officers often acknowledge awareness of such searches.

An extreme example of harassment involves a person "known" to be a pimp, for whom officers A and B "put on an act." In the presence of the "pimp" A became so emotional about his hatred for pimps that B had to restrain him physically. A took out his gun and said he was going to kill the "pimp," but B managed to keep A under control. B finally persuaded A to leave, but in parting, A said that next time he'll kill the "pimp." Then B quietly confided in the "pimp" that B feared he could not keep A under control, that A was emotionally unstable and probably would use his gun if the "pimp" did not move out of the district. Yet B promised to try to provide protection for the "pimp." The system worked, says the officer, for the "pimp" moved to another district. Supervisory officers of whom we inquired expressed verbal disapproval but seemed amused. They did not say they would issue orders not to engage in any such harassment.

The purposeful harassment that has come to light in our interviews may be widespread and frequent, or the examples we have learned about may be rather exceptional. I think our interviews do not provide a suffi-

Ch. 1   *ENFORCEMENT POLICY*

cient basis for making an appraisal of the significance of purposeful harassment, but they clearly support a recommendation that the Chicago police should make their own investigation.

**Prostitution.**

Most police action against prostitutes is under the "loitering prostitute" ordinance, not under the Illinois statute which requires much more evidence and is therefore much more difficult to enforce. Officers in the 21 police districts are the primary enforcers of the ordinance. The 18th district alone has 8 officers who spend full time on prostitution. The 25 officers of the prostitution section of the vice-control division limit themselves almost entirely to trying to enforce the statute, not the ordinance.

A key fact is that the maximum penalty for violating the ordinance is a $200 fine, even for those who have been convicted many times. Any weekday morning one can see 25 to 50 prostitutes waiting in Judge Cerda's court for their cases to be called; about 90% are black. They put up $100 for $1,000 bonds. The judge usually continues each case many times. The women weary of coming back over and over during hours they customarily sleep, and they pay more

## ENFORCEMENT POLICY  Ch. 1

money in forfeited bonds than in fines, perhaps much more, but Judge Cerda declines to make any estimate. Since the city's total take is a trifling portion of their earnings, one may wonder whether the whole system of attempted control of streetwalkers has *any* deterrent effect. Probably the most serious effect is loss of time from an arrest during the profitable hours. Some of the officers estimate that Chicago has "a few thousand" prostitutes. After interviewing many officers, we continue to wonder whether the prostitutes would be more numerous or more active if the police did nothing.

The Chicago police express hatred for the pimps (those who knowingly receive money earned by prostitutes) and the panderers (those who for money arrange for a woman to practice prostitution), but they are mostly frustrated in getting evidence against them. Yet some officers purport to "know" all about some pimps, and they talk freely about them. They say the pimps are of two classes—those who use violence and threats, including beatings and sometimes even murder, to control their prostitutes, and those known as "lover boys" who use women's affections to keep them under control. The police say that no streetwalker can operate

Ch. 1   *ENFORCEMENT POLICY*

in Chicago independently of pimps. A newcomer who does not know she needs a pimp soon learns through violence or threats.

One would suppose that if an inexperienced newcomer quickly learns what pimp controls streetwalkers in a particular area of the city, the police could. But the police say that getting evidence of payments by prostitutes to pimps is usually impossible. They have had a little success by using policewomen as decoys, but they dislike subjecting women to the dangers, and they ask an interviewer: "Would you like your wife or girlfriend to do that kind of thing?" So the pimps go on reaping most of the prostitution money. Some get all the money a woman collects except for a meager amount for her living expenses. The woman often believes that the pimp is investing the money for her future.

The Internal Revenue Service is beginning to look covetously at the pimp money, and the Chicago officers are pleased with their new ally. A pimp who lives in Cadillac style may for that reason have to share with Uncle Sam, and the evidence the IRS agents get may be useful to the Chicago police.

The vice control division tries to track down the call girls, who usually outwit the officers. The call girls generally serve only those customers who are recommended by customers they trust. Of course, the officers in plain clothes pretend to be customers, but for any man to get the number of a call girl requires a good deal of ingenuity, the officers say. The police think they know all about streetwalkers and pimps but not much about call girls. They will not even try to estimate the number of call girls.

A man who patronizes a prostitute is as guilty as the woman under the loitering ordinance and he may be also guilty of violating the statute which specifically makes patronizing a prostitute a crime. But the officers never arrest the man—unless in some way he gives the officer a hard time. The officers typically sympathize with the clean and respectable businessman who is not at all a criminal but who simply wants and adventure he can't arrange at home. The same officers regard the prostitute as contemptible.

When an officer spots a prostitute on the street, he sometimes watches her until she picks up a man. Then he may ask the man if he knows the woman and may ask what they were talking about. Not many men can pass the test, and the officer gets the evidence he needs that the woman was "hus-

## Ch. 1   *ENFORCEMENT POLICY*

tling." The officer arrests the woman but not the man, although no more effort would be required to arrest both. Can such a police policy be justified under an equal protection clause? My answer is that it probably cannot, but the reality of the law is not in what courts say about the Constitution; it is more often in what the enforcement officers do or don't do.

Some questions of policy, questions of fact, and mixed questions of policy and fact are either answered by the Chicago police on the basis of offhand and superficial thinking, are answered through neglect and drift, or are unanswered. Here are ten questions that I think might well be answered through investigations, studies, and give and take among those affected or interested:

1. How much of taxpayers' money is spent annually on control of prostitutes? If it is between one million and one and a half million, as it may be, what are the estimated benefits, who gets them, and what are they worth?

2. What portion of streetwalkers' time and earnings are consumed by enforcement? If a good estimate is in the neighborhood of five percent of each, does the enforcement provide *any* deterrence?

3. If the police are free to adopt a nonenforcement policy with respect to men who violate, as the Chicago police assume they are, does an equal freedom exist to adopt a nonenforcement policy with respect to streetwalkers or call girls or both?

4. Under existing legislation, would whatever interests are served by enforcement be better served, and would the costs of enforcement be reduced, if the police were to designate geographical areas of nonenforcement, coupled with full protection of other areas?

5. Would the enforcement policy be improved if all or most resources now devoted to call girls were transferred to control of pimps? The police themselves seem to regard their control of pimps as inadequate, but the lieutenant in charge of the prostitution section blames the statute for making enforcement too difficult. Yet he knows of no recommendation to the legislature for a change in the statute. If he is right, do the police have a responsibility for recommending such a change? The officers we have interviewed, including top officers of the department, sometimes make recommendations for changing legislation, but apparently not on questions of enforcement policy.

Ch. 1   *ENFORCEMENT POLICY*

6. Can the expenditures to control call girls be justified by a cost-benefit analysis? To the slight extent that call girls are caught and convicted, who gets the benefit, what is the benefit, and how much is it worth? Do businessmen who want to attract conventions to Chicago gain or lose from enforcement against call girls?

7. If enforcement against pimps were multiplied by ten or twenty through the employment of and proper protection of large numbers of policewomen, might the operation easily pass a cost-benefit test in that crimes believed to be committed by pimps would be reduced?

8. Does existing legislation about streetwalkers need to be changed, and do the police have responsibility for recommending statutory amendments? The principal law used against streetwalkers is an ordinance authorizing a maximum penalty of $200, and even that penalty is seldom imposed. For instance, the records of Judge Cerda's prostitution cases for June, 1974, show from the 18th district no fines, 127 discharges, and 32 cases pending; from the 19th district, 8 fines, 47 discharges, and 50 pending. Of the few fines, some are $25. The continuances are so numerous that one wonders whether

*ENFORCEMENT POLICY* Ch. 1

the system is primarily one of harassment, not one of imposing punishing on those found guilty. If the system is unsatisfactory, do the police have a primary responsibility for getting it changed? The officers we have interviewed do not seem to think so.

9. Under existing legislation, can venereal testing be required of every prostitute taken into custody? If so, should the police impose the requirement? Should the police release a prostitute who is spreading the disease? The present answers seem unsatisfactory; a judge, without explicit statutory authority, requires of alleged prostitutes a certificate of venereal testing that is not more than three months old, and one who supplies such a certificate may be spreading the disease and may go on doing so. Do the police have a responsibility to deal with this problem, either by taking action or by recommending legislation?

10. Should the police make studies and investigations to answer all such questions of policy and of fact as those listed above? Should the police employ lawyers and sociologists to help with such studies and investigations?

## Ch. 1   ENFORCEMENT POLICY

**Informers.**

The Chicago police have an elaborate set of practices about the use of informers to assist in law enforcement. Through their practices they answer such questions of policy as these: Should any offender be given a chance to earn immunity from punishment by giving information to the police? Should the police buy information about law violators by paying money? Should they buy such information with non-arrest, with non-prosecution, or with non-punishment? Is it a denial of equal protection to give a chance to one violator to become an informer but not to give a similar chance to another? Should all violators have such a chance, and if not, on what basis should selections be made? Should one who is caught selling narcotics be given immunity from prosecution for burglary if he gives the police valuable information about big narcotics distributors? On what grounds may a valuable informer status be terminated? Is the informer entitled to fair procedure when termination of his informer status is under consideration? If the police renege on promises they have made to an informer, should the informer have a legal remedy? Is the entire structure of police informer practices illegal for lack of statutory authorization; if so,

*ENFORCEMENT POLICY* Ch. 1

who, if anyone, can get the question before a court?

Officers at a low level now seem to have absolute power to decide who may and who may not become an informer. The basis for decision as to which guilty person goes to jail and which one is traded a freedom from jail in return for information may be wholly capricious and may depend mainly on emotional reactions to particular personalities. One who is the victim of an unfavorable decision has no practical remedy.

The police sometimes trade non-arrest for information, but that practice is usually though not always limited to misdemeanors; yet some arrests for burglary have been withheld on the ground that the burglar is an informer. Some officers say they have refrained from investigating some felonies when they believe the offender is an informer. The main system is one of holding out to a guilty person that if he supplies sufficient information to the police, they will write a "letter of consideration" to the state's attorney, asking for "consideration" of the information the individual has given the police. Such letters are used far more in narcotics violations than in any other class of case, and since the state's attorney's office handles from 200 to 300 narcotics cas-

## Ch. 1   *ENFORCEMENT POLICY*

es each week, such a letter virtually guarantees dismissal of the case. So the decision that matters is made by the police.

When an informer does his best and produces valuable information, but the police happen to have that information from other sources, should he be rewarded? Some officers write the letter of consideration and some do not. When an informer fulfills half his bargain and tries to fulfill the rest, should he be rewarded? The answer is both yes and no, without rhyme or reason. The police do often pay money for information; when partial performance is insufficient for a letter of consideration, should money be paid? The answer is that no money is paid in such circumstances; either the partial performance is rewarded with a letter of consideration or it is not rewarded.

Should letters of consideration be limited to misdemeanors or should they also reach felonies? They do apply to felonies; sale of narcotics is a felony, and a letter of consideration often applies to such sales. Should letters of consideration apply to homicide, armed robbery, and rape? The answer is no, but they do apply to burglary. Some officers say the line is drawn between burglary that involves danger to life and burglary of an empty house, but others say no such line exists; the question is apparently for the discretion of the officer in the particular case. In at least one instance, non-arrest for burglary was traded for information, but in many cases letters of consideration have been written for burglars. When a burglar led the police to 15 pounds of heroin, every officer was quite clear that he had earned a letter of consideration.

May one who supplies a steady stream of information go on committing crimes indefinitely and always be protected by letters of consideration? The police are uncomfortable about this question and seem to agree that some cutoff point needs to be located, but no such point has been established.

An addict who gains an informer status may continue his sales and supply his own needs as long as he provides the information that is expected of him. But he has no protection against capricious termination of his status. A single officer may seemingly hold the vital interests of a number of human beings in the palm of his hand, with no rules to guide him and no superior authority to check him.

# CHAPTER 2

# HOW THE POLICE MAKE ENFORCEMENT POLICY

## Research and development.

When I learned that the Chicago police have a research and development unit, I went there and promptly found an office labeled "Policy Development and Program Evaluation." But the occupant had nothing to do with that subject. He explained: "Those words simply haven't been taken down since O. W. Wilson put them up. We haven't had any policy development or program evaluation since he retired."

That remark summarizes what top officers do about enforcement policy. The general orders and the special orders—the only written directives from the superintendent to others in the department—seldom mention enforcement policy, and nearly all of them studiously avoid any acknowledgment that any statute or ordinance may be properly left unenforced on any occasion. One can read all the general orders, special orders, and training bulletins without learning that selective enforcement exists, except

[*32*]

that one training bulletin speaks of selective enforcement with respect to traffic offenses, and occasional instructions are given to enforce "with restraint and discretion."

The unit that is called "research and development" has nothing to do with what I would consider to be research. It does not tackle difficult sociological problems. The director's answer to my question whether any research is done on enforcement policy was in one word: "No." The big "research" project this year has been designing policewomen's uniforms. A study has been made of alternative methods of paying for overtime, and of advantages and disadvantages of painting all police cars yellow. A continuing job of the 34 people in the unit is keeping crime statistics up to date, but they also deal with forms and records, technology, uniforms and equipment, and federal programs. A general order says the unit "conducts management studies involving organization, methods and procedures with the objective of increasing the effectiveness of Department operations," but the current director remembers no such study.

**The ingredients of enforcement policy.**

Obviously, many substantive factors enter into policymaking, including training, expe-

## Ch. 2  HOW POLICY IS MADE

rience, values, information, pressures, personalities, and politics. But anyone who interviews the Chicago police on the subject of selective enforcement will be quickly convinced that two other ingredients are so dominant as to be in a class by themselves. Almost every officer explains any particular selective enforcement policy by relying on one or the other of the two items. The two main ingredients of all law enforcement policy of the Chicago police, according to the officers we interviewed, are (1) the obligation to enforce all law and (2) lack of resources to enforce all law. When the police enforce the law, the reason they always give is that they have the obligation to enforce it. When they do not enforce the law, their reason is that they can't enforce all law. In interviewing at any level of the Chicago police, one has great difficulty getting any officer to balance one of the two reasons against the other. Intelligent and experienced officers who are fully aware that much law is unenforced solemnly assert the ritual that they are required to enforce all law. That ritual makes explanations easy. *But it is a major source of confused thinking.*

The confusion about the obligation to enforce and the lack of resources to enforce seems to apply to all subjects that involve some degree of nonenforcement. A good example is the policy about pornography. The policy is one of enforcing in such a way that sellers go on selling. An interview with the principal maker of the policy ran something like this:

"Why do you enforce at all?"

"Because selling pornography is a crime."

"Then why not enforce enough to cut down the sale?"

"Because we can't commit that much manpower to something that does so little harm."

"Then why not save the manpower you now use?"

"Because the statute makes it a crime."

"Does anyone get any benefit from the partial enforcement?"

"Yes, some money is collected in fines."

"Do the fines compensate for the expenses of police, prosecutors, and courts?"

"I don't know. We don't think in such terms."

"Apart from the fines, does anyone get any benefit from the partial enforcement?"

## Ch. 2  *HOW POLICY IS MADE*

"That's not for us to decide. The legislative body has made the sale of pornography a crime, and that's enough."

"Then is it accurate to say that you reject a policy of full enforcement, you reject a policy of nonenforcement, and you adopt a policy of occasional enforcement, without considering the question whether enforcement is desirable?"

"Well, we can't commit more manpower, and the statute requires us to do what we can to enforce."

My impression from talking with the maker of the policy is that he has made a judgment as to how much manpower should be committed to the subject but that that is as far as his policy thinking goes. If his mind were set free from the unquestioning belief that he has an obligation to enforce all laws and ordinances, he could then think about what the policy should be. He could then think in terms of a cost-benefit analysis of what the police are doing. And then he might find that the expenditure the police now make for control of pornography has little or nothing on the benefit side of the ledger. The police program increases the annual cost of doing business in the average amount of about $540 in fines, but does it cut down the sale of pornography?

The myth of full enforcement—a major ingredient in policymaking—is harmful, for it confuses the makers of policy. The quality of the thinking that goes into the policy will be improved if the policymakers are free to decide what the policy should be, after considering the pros and cons of each question.

The third most important ingredient of policymaking, after the obligation to enforce and the limited enforcement resources, is probably the police officers' impressions and misimpressions about prosecutors' and judges' policies and practices. A startling proportion of police policy is based on facts and myths about law and legal processes. The ways of prosecutors and judges are somewhat mysterious to many policemen, and a good deal of policy is based on assumptions that may be mistaken. For instance, officers generally say they will not arrest for attempted bribery, even if witnesses are present; the reason, they usually say, is that the courts don't convict for attempted bribery. Yet no officer interviewed on the question has been able to mention a case of refusal to convict when witnesses in

Ch. 2   *HOW POLICY IS MADE*

addition to the officer testified to the attempted bribery. The policy does not depend on facts; it depends on beliefs, some which may be mistaken. Of course, judges and prosecutors are sometimes largely responsible for police misunderstandings.

**The role of patrolmen in making policy.**

Top officers seem to have little to do with the making of enforcement policy. Some of the policy is made by officers of middle grade, but most of it is made at the bottom of the organization by ordinary patrolmen. Much of the enforcement policy is not known by top officers, and some of it is at variance with what the top officers think it should be. Yet when policy made by patrolmen is called to the attention of high officers who express their disagreement with it, the high officers are seldom inclined to do anything about the policy.

The patterns followed when patrolmen are the main makers of enforcement policy vary a bit in their detail, especially in degree of uniformity of the policy, in degree of agreement or disagreement of superior officers, and in degree of interference or participation by superior officers. A good example to inspect carefully is the policy about arresting for smoking marijuana in public.

## HOW POLICY IS MADE   Ch. 2

Possession of any quantity of marijuana is a crime according to the statute. But patrolmen are nearly unanimous in not arresting one who is smoking a marijuana cigaret. That patrolmen are the ones who make the policy is shown by the fact that nearly all supervisory officers—sergeants and above—say they believe the arrest should be made. But district commanders and watch commanders are quite clear that they are not inclined to require their men to make the arrest. The patrolmen remain free to make their own policy. Some of the supervisory officers acknowledge that they do not know what the policy is. Nearly all the patrolmen have the same policy; they seem generally informed about what other patrolmen are doing. And nearly all of them give the same reasons; they say no one will be convicted for possessing a small quantity of marijuana, and that making the arrest would take them off the streets for two or three hours to do the paperwork and process the arrest, since all narcotics evidence must be handcarried to headquarters.

Another facet of enforcement concerning marijuana is an illustration of a policy that varies from one patrolman to another: The patrolmen who were interviewed differed widely on what specific quantity of marijuana should be enough to justify an arrest. Higher officers had their own ideas but did not know what the policy is, and some did not know that the answer differs from one officer to another.

The various harassment policies are made almost entirely by patrolmen, sometimes with the knowledge of their superiors but generally without the superiors' disapproval. Yet the superiors often assert in interviews that they disagree. The system of harassing by arresting for disorderly conduct those who have in no sense been disorderly is strongly disapproved by some superiors— verbally in interviews but not in firm orders issued to subordinates. The policy of harassing "known" criminals by frequently stopping and questioning them is usually approved and encouraged by superiors, but the policy stems from patrolmen, who give it their own twists. Policies about not taking into custody juveniles who have committed minor crimes are made wholly by patrolmen and vary widely from one patrolman to another; the nonarrest policies are not necessarily the same as those of the youth officers who decide questions about stationhouse adjustment for juveniles.

## Professional staffs and special studies.

A key fact about the Chicago police is that they do not employ professional staffs and that they do not make special studies of problems of enforcement policy. An advanced administrative agency has specialists trained in many disciplines, and the agency assigns facets of its major problems to the appropriate specialists for making studies and reports. Then tentative drafts of policy positions are put together and are subjected to many kinds of criticism, both inside and outside the agency. When rules are prepared, proposed rules are published and an opportunity is given to private parties who are affected to send in written comments and arguments.

The Chicago police have no professional staffs, no special studies of enforcement policy problems, no tentative drafts of policy positions, no procedure for getting written comments from affected parties.

Strangely, enforcement policy is not made in the name of the superintendent. The general orders and special orders issued by him deal hardly at all with enforcement policy. Nearly all such policy is made by patrolmen, and the rest of it is made by officers of middle grade.

## Ch. 2   HOW POLICY IS MADE

One of my early interviews was with an officer I shall not identify, who is now in a higher position. He was once the head of a section (other than the prostitution section). He proudly told me that a few days after he was appointed, he had his enforcement policy all formulated, and he told me what it was. Instead of admiring his promptness and decisiveness, as he seemingly expected me to do, I inquired with a tone of consternation: "Do you mean that in a few days you single-handedly made the whole policy without consulting anyone inside or outside the department?" He responded: "Of course I did. That was my job. I was the section head. I had to make the policy." He agreed with me that others within the department might have ideas differing from his, but he saw no reason for consultation. I explained to him that in a good federal agency such policymaking would be the subject of much group work, with give and take, special studies by appropriate professionals, and reworking of tentative drafts on the basis of many kinds of criticism. He said that police work is different. The best way to make police policy, he said, is for one officer to take the responsibility and to decide what he wants.

He is surely right that the way the police make policy is different from the way a good federal agency makes it. Of course, the question I want to raise is whether the federal agency's way is better. I am convinced that it is. The police way reflects the fiction, which seemingly is always in the forefront of police minds, that "We just enforce the law. We don't make policy." The former section head knew he was making policy—he even called it "my policy"—but he was still governed by the absence of policymaking machinery, an absence that stems largely from the lingering belief that "We just enforce the law."

The worst part of the answer to the question of who makes police policy is that professional people with specialized training seldom participate. Policies are made that call for answers to legal questions, sociological questions, and psychological questions, but the questions in such fields usually are not even raised, for no lawyers, sociologists, or psychologists are available to answer them. The President's Crime Commission found in 1967 that the police have an average education of 12.4 years; if most policy is made by patrolmen, and if all higher officers are excluded, most policy must be made by those

Ch. 2   *HOW POLICY IS MADE*

with substantially less than 12.4 years in school.

The absence of legal advisers within the Chicago police department seems to me especially unfortunate. The ways of lawyers and judges seem mysterious to the ordinary patrolman. Misimpressions are rather common. The policy of nonarrest even for a serious crime when the victim refuses to sign a complaint is probably attributable in the main to a misimpression on the part of patrolmen about legal processes.

Clearly the Chicago police need ready access to legal advisers. They have no such access now. The department has many officers who have legal training—one estimate is about fifty—but they are doing nonlegal work. The theory that the corporation counsel or the state's attorney advises the police is contrary to the usual fact. Thanks to funding by the Law Enforcement Assistance Administration, the police of the nation had 254 legal advisers as of December, 1973, and the number is rapidly growing. The New York City police department added 23 legal advisers to its staff during 1973. But Chicago has not obtained LEAA money for legal advisers. It should.

Dallas experience throws light on potentialities. Mr. Edwin Heath is the legal adviser. Seven lawyers work under him within the Dallas police force. His complaint is that he needs more assistants; the amount of legal work to be done is too much for eight lawyers. The main function of the legal adviser and his staff is to answer inquiries of policemen—mainly telephone calls—as to what to do about an immediate problem. Mr. Heath takes pride in giving clear answers to all questions, even when the law is unclear and even when the lawyer knows of no relevant law; his theory is that the guess of the lawyer on a legal question is likely to be better than the guess of the nonlawyer.

The Chicago police seem quite primitive in continuing their longstanding custom of deciding legal questions without the help of lawyers, deciding questions in other professional fields without the help of the appropriate professional people, and resolving difficult and complex problems of enforcement policy without special studies by qualified staffs.

My opinion is that the police themselves need to upgrade the level of their activities. They tend to emphasize the physical processes. They regard their work as merely ministerial. "We just enforce the law."

## Ch. 2 *HOW POLICY IS MADE*

Their self-image is one that unduly diminishes the discretionary and policy-making tasks. Police work calls for a good deal of thinking about difficult and complex problems. The attitude that it does not is at variance with the reality. Yet, even in my talks with the top six officers, the superintendent and the five deputy superintendents, I was struck with the resistance to the idea that their work can and should be on a higher professional plane. I think they hurt themselves by maintaining their attitude. More importantly, I think they hurt those they serve.

**Procedure.**

The principal procedure by which the Chicago police make enforcement policy is by leaving patrolmen free to make policy as they encounter problems in their patrol. Such policy is based mainly on guesswork and superficial impressions. Many policy decisions by patrolmen are guided by experience, observation, thoughtfulness, and understanding, but many are not. Some are based on misunderstanding, such as the belief that one cannot be convicted without voluntary testimony of the victim.

Top officers do not delegate policymaking power to their subordinates. Instead, the top officers simply do nothing about most problems of enforcement policy, so that when patrolmen are confronted with the problems they resolve them as best they can. The unrecorded habits of patrolmen make up the great bulk of police enforcement policy. The policy the patrolmen make is seldom reviewed by superiors and much of it is unknown to them.

What the policymaking procedure is seems to me less significant than what it is not. It is not based on studies. It is not based on the work of professionals. It is not a product of systematic give and take. It is not submitted to critics inside and outside the department with a solicitation of their ideas. Those affected have no opportunity to comment on proposed policies. Since 1946 a federal statute has required federal agencies to follow what has come to be known as "notice and comment" procedures for some of their rulemaking. The police we have interviewed, including top officers, have never heard of any such procedure and most of them reject it out of hand, without trying to understand its potentialities. Yet a few of the top officers have manifested some interest in the idea that some enforcement policies might be embodied in proposed rules that would be published and opened up for public comment.

## Coordination with other organs of government.

The totality of governmental policymaking concerning law enforcement involves four classes of participants: Legislators determine what acts are criminal, usually with little or no regard for what is or is not enforceable; the police often decide through nonenforcement to cut back what legislators make criminal; the prosecutors pick and choose among violators whose cases come to them through the police; and the judges make their own policies about convicting or not convicting, and about punishing or not punishing.

The four types of public servants operate largely in separate compartments, with little or no coordination. On some problems, everyone thinks someone else has the primary responsibility. The superintendent told me that he sometimes has conferences with prosecutors and judges, but when I asked him what conference he has had with prosecutors and judges about law enforcement policy, he acknowledged that he has had none. I do not have a comprehensive view of what can be accomplished through better coordination, but I see a good many signs of the need for that.

The pornography policy is an example. The legislators have provided for imprisonment not to exceed one year or a fine not to exceed $1,000, or both, for a first offense, and up to three years and $5,000 for a second or subsequent offense, but the legislators have not prescribed the enforcement policies of police, prosecutors, or judges. The police generally do not arrest managers or owners because, some of them say, proving scienter is too difficult. So the police arrest only the clerk who sells a particular magazine or pamphlet. Since only a clerk is involved, the judge almost never imposes imprisonment. The result of the unplanned system is that the proprietor of a store that sells pornography has to pay an average annual fine of about $540. Whether the legislative policy should be to deter selling of pornography I do not know, but if it is, I think a four-way conference of legislators, police, prosecutors, and judges could consider what the policy should be, including the enforcement policy. The idea of such a conference on enforcement policy is a radical one, for the Chicago police have apparently never tried it. Probably the one pornography policy that should *not* be chosen at such

Ch. 2   *HOW POLICY IS MADE*

a conference is the one the police now have —to spend police resources on control of pornography while accomplishing nothing by way of deterrence.

Although judges do not confer with administrative officers about judicial decisions in particular cases, I see no reason why judges should not participate in conferences with legislators, police, and prosecutors about overall questions of policy, when the policy is administered by judges, prosecutors, and police. A conference on such a subject could even be appropriately open— open to the press and open to the public. The failure here may be largely or mostly that of the judges. When O. W. Wilson sought a conference with Chicago judges, they agreed to meet with him on condition that they would not discuss court or police business! They seemed to think they would lose their objectivity by conferring with the police about police business.

**Summary.**

On the basis of what has been said above in this chapter, my opinion is that the methods by which the Chicago police make enforcement policy are grossly deficient in five respects: (1) The top officers fail to make most of the policy, so that patrolmen become the primary makers of the policy. (2) No one in the department makes special studies for the purpose of formulating policy. The policy choices are usually based on nothing better than patrolmen's offhand judgments. (3) The department does not employ professional staffs who have the requisite training in various fields. The department does not even have a staff of legal advisers. (4) The department has no administrative procedure for ascertaining preferences of the community about enforcement policy or for allowing members of the public to know and to criticize the department's enforcement policy. (5) The department makes no effort to coordinate its enforcement policy with the policy of prosecutors and judges, and some of its enforcement policy is based on misimpressions of the policy of prosecutors and judges.

# CHAPTER 3

# THE PERVASIVE FALSE PRETENSE OF FULL ENFORCEMENT

**The overall picture.**

The five gross deficiencies in the methods by which the Chicago police make enforcement policy, just summarized in the concluding section of the preceding chapter, all stem directly from the pervasive system of falsely pretending that all statutes and ordinances are fully enforced. The police assume that full enforcement is required by an Illinois statute and by four Chicago ordinances, and when either insufficient resources or good sense requires nonenforcement they also assume that they must do what they can to conceal the nonenforcement. So the only open enforcement policy is one of full enforcement. The top officers accordingly assume that they never have any enforcement policy to make. So they do not make enforcement policy. The false pretense thus causes the patrolmen to become the primary makers of policy, for when they are confronted with an enforcement problem, they cannot escape a decision to act or not to act.

*PRETENDED FULL ENFORCEMENT* Ch. 3

Because of the false pretense of full enforcement, no studies are ever made to guide the formulation of enforcement policy, and no professional staffs are ever needed for that purpose. And because the police falsely pretend to have no enforcement policy except one of full enforcement, no occasion arises for ascertaining community desires about enforcement policy, or for coordinating police enforcement policy with the policy of prosecutors and judges.

The false pretense of full enforcement has all these devastating consequences. It is a central and pervasive reality, especially in the minds of all officers above the patrolman level. The pretense of full enforcement is a prominent part of what officers have said to us in our interviews with 300 of them. **For** the typical officer, especially supervisory officers, the pretense relieves him from the work of directly addressing his mind to questions of enforcement policy, since such questions may be so easily assumed to be already resolved in favor of full enforcement on all occasions.

The false pretense has not been created by the present personnel of the Chicago police department. They have inherited it. It probably started during the second half of

## Ch. 3 *PRETENDED FULL ENFORCEMENT*

the nineteenth century and may have been full-blown by 1900. Everyone now in the department grew up on it and has naturally assumed it ever since.

The cause of the false pretense is clearly the combination of full enforcement legislation (statutes and ordinances) with the lack of resources for full enforcement and the common sense of some nonenforcement.

This chapter discusses the full enforcement legislation, and then describes the accomplishment of patrolmen in departing from that legislation. The story is largely one of police wisdom in escaping from the full enforcement legislation, but with extreme damage from the supposed necessity for concealing the truth about enforcement policy. I shall analyze that damage, and then I shall present the reasons for disclosing enforcement practices. In the next chapter, a legal analysis will show the legality of an open system of selective enforcement, which is what I strongly recommend.

### The full enforcement legislation.

The Illinois revised statutes of 1845 imposed the duty on every constable, when a crime was committed in his presence, "forthwith to apprehend the person" and bring

*PRETENDED FULL ENFORCEMENT* Ch. 3

him before some justice of the peace. In 1874 the statute was expanded to cover "every . . . policeman." The present provision is ch. 125, § 82: "It shall be the duty of every sheriff, coroner, and every marshal, policeman, or other officer of any incorporated city, town or village, having the power of a sheriff, when any criminal offense or breach of the peace is committed or attempted in his presence, forthwith to apprehend the offender and bring him before some judge, to be dealt with according to law . . . ." The statute has been interpreted to apply to misdemeanors as well as felonies, People v. Davies, 354 Ill. 168, 188 N.E. 337 (1934), but no other judicial interpretation relevant to the present context has been found.

The duty imposed by that statute is combined with ch. 38, § 33–3: "A public officer or employee commits misconduct when, in his official capacity, he commits any of the following acts: (a) Intentionally or recklessly fails to perform any mandatory duty as required by law. . . . A public officer or employee convicted of violating any provision of this Section forfeits his office or employment." In addition, he is subject to fine and to imprisonment up to five years in the penitentiary.

## Ch. 3 *PRETENDED FULL ENFORCEMENT*

The Chicago Municipal Code contains four ordinances which call for full enforcement by the police. One is § 11–9, which provides that the police board "shall, through the Superintendent of Police . . . enforce all laws, ordinances of the city and orders of the City Council and of the Mayor." Whatever applies to the superintendent must apply to all the police, since he acts through them. A second ordinance is § 11–24: "The members of the police force of the city, when on duty, shall devote their time and attention to the discharge of the duties of their stations, according to the laws of the state and ordinances of the city and the rules and regulations of the department, to preserve order, peace, and quiet and enforce the laws and ordinances throughout the city." Even if the provision may be properly read to mean that "The members . . . shall . . . enforce the laws and ordinances . . ." that meaning seems a bit unclear. But the provision clearly says that the members shall devote their time to discharge of their duties according to the laws of the state, and the Illinois statute imposes the "duty" to apprehend an offender for a crime committed or attempted in the presence of an officer. The ordinance also requires discharge of duties

[56]

*PRETENDED FULL ENFORCEMENT* Ch. 3

according to "rules and regulations of the department" and those rules and regulations require full enforcement, as we shall shortly see.

A third ordinance, § 11–31, provides: "Any member of the police force who shall refuse or neglect to perform any duty required of him, when such refusal or neglect to perform any such duty shall tend to hinder, obstruct, or impair in any way the proper and strict enforcement of any law or provision of this code or the efficiency of the police force, is hereby declared to be no longer qualified to be a member of the police force, and shall be discharged from said police force and the service of the city in the manner provided by law." The key word is "duty," and again the meaning depends on the Illinois statute and on the department's rules and regulations.

And the same is true of the fourth ordinance, § 11–32: "Any member of the police department who shall neglect or refuse to perform any duty required of him by the provisions of this code or the rules and regulations of the department of police . . . may, in addition to any other penalty or punishment imposed by law, be fined not more than one hundred dollars for each offense."

Ch. 3 *PRETENDED FULL ENFORCEMENT*

One cannot escape the conclusion that the four ordinances, even though they are dependent on the statute and on the regulations, say rather clearly that the police have an obligation to enforce all statutes and ordinances. The statute and the ordinances together will be referred to as "the full enforcement legislation."

## Formal administrative action supporting the full enforcement legislation.

The formal (but not the actual) power to make rules and regulations to govern the department is not in the department but is in the Chicago police board, which, in December of 1973, issued a 34-page printed pamphlet entitled "Chicago Police Department— Rules and Regulations." Part II states six "goals of the department," the fourth of which is "Enforcement of all laws and ordinances." Part V, on "rules of conduct," states 55 "prohibited acts," the third of which is "any failure to promote the Department's efforts to implement its policy or accomplish its goals." Part VI states penalties for violating the rules and regulations—oral reprimand, written reprimand, extra duty without compensation, suspension without pay, and institution of charges before the police board. The rules and regulations thus

*PRETENDED FULL ENFORCEMENT* Ch. 3

mean that all officers have a duty to "enforce all laws and ordinances." That is clearly the formal enforcement policy.

Formal instructions from the superintendent to his subordinates are in the form of "general orders," "special orders," and to some extent "training bulletins." General order 70–4, issued in 1970, is on the subject of "district watch commanders." It provides in part III: "The district watch commander will . . . direct the enforcement of all laws and ordinances and the rules, regulations, and orders of the Department during his tour of duty." The general order contains no exception to the words "all laws and ordinances."

Another example is general order 70–10, also issued in 1970 (but now repealed), on the subject of "district vice officers." It provided in part III, B: "The duties of district vice officers will include the enforcement of all statutes and ordinances relating to gambling, prostitution, narcotics, and liquor laws . . ." No exception to the words "all statutes and ordinances" was mentioned.

One wonders about possible negative implications of some orders. For instance, patrolmen are unanimous in refusing to arrest

[59]

## Ch. 3 *PRETENDED FULL ENFORCEMENT*

for social gambling in absence of complaint or unusual circumstance, and the superiors are well aware of that policy. No general order even mentions social gambling. But general order 73–10, issued in 1973, is on the subject of "lottery gambling enforcement program," and the first sentence is: "This order . . . continues an intensified enforcement program aimed at eliminating lottery gambling." Would a perceptive officer know that an order to bear down on lotteries may mean that bearing down on other forms of gambling is not stressed?

Officers we have interviewed have often told us that the policy of the department has always been to avoid any statement in writing that directs or authorizes any officer to engage in nonenforcement in any circumstances. Even a deputy superintendent has said to me explicitly that superior officers never instruct subordinates not to enforce. Our search of the general orders and special orders almost completely supports that statement. Exceptions are very slight. A training bulletin, III, 38, issued in 1962, has one sentence that seems to authorize nonenforcement: "The keynotes in the enforcement of any curfew ordinance are the application of common sense and good judgment." A training bulletin on traffic violators,

*PRETENDED FULL ENFORCEMENT* Ch. 3

VII, 10, 1966, provides: "In consideration of the safety of others, it may be more practical to allow a traffic violator to escape rather than jeopardize others in a high-speed chase." Another traffic enforcement training bulletin, VII, 48, 1966, is unusually daring when it says that "you will be selective in your enforcement. You can then patrol an area at the time accidents are happening, at the locations where they occur and be able to observe the violations that cause them." See also another training bulletin, VIII, 26, 1967.

We spent a good deal of time interviewing in the training division of the department, but we found no attempt to teach selective enforcement policy. The absence of such instruction was finally confirmed by interviews with instructors and with recruits. Some of the instruction affirmatively emphasizes the policy of full enforcement. The recruit has to learn about nonenforcement from his colleagues after he is on the job. Yet a recruit is exposed to nonenforcement if he reads The Challenge of Crime in a Free Society, as he is supposed to do. Some nonenforcement is inevitably mentioned in class discussions, as for example a discussion of how a juvenile gang fight at a high school dance was satisfactorily handled without an

Ch. 3 *PRETENDED FULL ENFORCEMENT*

arrest. A police woman trainee specifically said that in her training courses she had never heard a discussion of discretion not to arrest.

**The police accomplishment.**

The police generally realize but are reluctant to acknowledge that the legislative bodies have often overshot very considerably in enacting criminal legislation, and they may also realize that the legislative excesses are compounded by the full enforcement legislation. Nevertheless the rule of full enforcement is in the forefront of their minds: "We have an obligation to enforce everything." Even so, the legislative bodies lack the practical power to repeal the common sense of confident, secure, and experienced officers.

The common sense of the officers very often prevails over the legislative excesses in the criminal legislation, as compounded by the full enforcement legislation. That is the police accomplishment.

The second section of the first chapter of this essay contains "twenty quick samples of nonenforcement of criminal statutes and ordinances." All twenty of those samples are relevant here. No matter what the legislative body has made a crime and no matter what the literal words of the full enforcement legislation say, patrolmen do not arrest for all offenses committed in their presence. Patrolmen are in fact often lenient. They know that some legislation is almost never enforced, and they know that common sense requires that it be almost never enforced. Even when the crime is committed in their presence, they do not ordinarily arrest for such crimes as fornication in a public park, quiet drinking in the park, smoking in an elevator, spitting on the sidewalk, or social gambling with a friend. Patrolmen ordinarily refrain from making such arrests, in absence of special reasons to make them, despite the words of the ordinance that an officer who fails to perform such a duty is "no longer qualified to be a member of the police force, and shall be discharged from said police force." That is, I think, a police accomplishment.

Let us consider for a moment some examples of police leniency toward normal children, in violation of the literal terms of the full enforcement legislation. A 9-year-old lights a firecracker for which he has just traded some marbles. Should the patrolman, no matter what the circumstances, take him into custody? He is required to if he follows the literal meaning of the full enforcement legislation. A 12-year-old gets a

## Ch. 3 *PRETENDED FULL ENFORCEMENT*

new bicycle and promptly rides it on the sidewalk, in violation of an ordinance applying to anyone 12 years old or more. Should the patrolman explain the ordinance to him and not take him into custody for the first offense? A 13-year-old, by rare good marksmanship, throws a rock forty yards and breaks the only unbroken window in an abandoned building, and is therefore technically guilty of vandalism. A 14-year-old is guilty of an offense when his older friends first introduce him to beer. A 16-year-old brings his girl friend home a little too late and violates the curfew laws, which make no exceptions for human circumstances.

The police spend more than half their law enforcement time on minor crimes, and some minor crimes are rather puny ones that clearly do not call for full enforcement on all occasions. An ordinance, § 193–7.10, makes it a crime to smoke in "any street car, elevated train, or subway," and imposes a penalty of not more than $5. The superintendent of the Chicago police told me that the evening before we were talking he had asked a fellow passenger in an elevated train to put out his cigaret; the man refused until the superintendent identified himself. What the superintendent said indirectly was that he did not apprehend one who was commit-

*PRETENDED FULL ENFORCEMENT* Ch. 3

ting a crime in his presence. Should he have apprehended the man, or should he have used his own good judgment, as he did? The fact is that he did not do his "duty" under ch. 125, § 82, for he did not "apprehend the offender and bring him before some judge." The superintendent violated ch. 38, § 33–3, for which the penalty may be imprisonment up to five years. He failed under § 11–9 of the ordinances to "enforce all . . . ordinances . . . ." Under § 11–31 he is "no longer qualified to be a member of the police force." And he violated his "duty" under the police board's formal rules and regulations to "enforce all . . . ordinances" and is therefore subject to discharge.

What utter nonsense! Could any rational legislative body have possibly intended any such results? The police accomplishment in escaping the full enforcement legislation is a very considerable one, for which the police deserve much credit.

The system of criminal justice would be insufferable without that police accomplishment.

Even though the police insist on interpreting the full enforcement legislation literally, they also insist on following what they re-

Ch. 3 *PRETENDED FULL ENFORCEMENT*

gard as their own common sense. This means that they violate their own interpretation of the full enforcement legislation. And I regard that as an accomplishment. *The police wisdom has on a wide scale overidden the legislative unwisdom embodied in the literal terms of the full enforcement legislation.* The police are properly lenient to many offenders. They do adapt their enforcement practices to the dominant community attitudes they are able to perceive. They do often refuse to make arrests for offenses committed in their presence. They have even established many patterns of nonenforcement.

**Three possible courses of action for the police.**

Confronted with their own literal interpretation of the full enforcement legislation, the police could theoretically follow any one of three possible courses of action: (1) Full enforcement in fact, along with truthful statement of it, (2) selective enforcement, along with pretense of full enforcement, and (3) selective enforcement, along with truthful statement of it. (A fourth possibility of full enforcement, along with a pretense of selective enforcement, is not worth considering.)

(1) In an ideal world, the first might be the best, if some leeway were left for discre-

tionary leniency. But in an ideal world, the criminal legislation would be tailored to what is practically enforceable, and our present legislation falls short by a wide margin. Either we must cut back the legislation or we must allow some nonenforcement of our excessive legislation—or a little of each. I favor cutting back the legislation, but I do not *expect* that. Our legislative bodies probably lack the capacity to legislate the needed refinement. The only practical way for legislative bodies to accomplish the objective of full enforcement is probably by delegating power to a rulemaking agency to cut back the excessive statutes to what can and should be enforced, and that agency might well be the police. Over a period of time the police could formulate rules that would be susceptible of full enforcement—if the rules contained enough vaguenesses and escape clauses to permit needed individualizing. But, as I show in chapter 5, the police already have that kind of rulemaking power, without an explicit delegation of it. If we start with the first of the three theoretical courses of action and make the necessary modifications in it, we wind up with the third one.

We cannot enforce our present legislation fully unless we cut it back either by amend-

## Ch. 3 *PRETENDED FULL ENFORCEMENT*

ing it or by changing it through rulemaking. The very idea of changing legislation through rulemaking sounds repugnant and obviously illegal—until one takes into account the expressions of legislative intent that are inconsistent with the legislation, and those expressions are set forth and analyzed in chapter 4.

The first course of action is the one we have tried over a period of more than a century, and no information has come to light that it works in even a single one of the 40,000 police agencies over the country. We know from experience that the first course does not work. That is why we apparently do not have it anywhere.

(2) What we have in Chicago is the same as what apparently all other American communities have—selective enforcement, along with the pretense of full enforcement. The Chicago police provide selective enforcement because they *cannot* provide full enforcement and because full enforcement often seems to them to be contrary to common sense. They pretend to have full enforcement because they interpret the full enforcement legislation literally. They assume they cannot tell the truth about their own practices. Yet many harms stem from their false pretense.

*PRETENDED FULL ENFORCEMENT* Ch. 3

(3) The only one of the three courses of action that can produce a satisfactory system is selective enforcement, along with truthful statement of it. We already have selective enforcement. The needed change is from falsity to truth, not merely because truth is in general preferable to falsity (as it surely is for a police agency) but because so many harms flow from the falsity.

The assumption of the Chicago police that falsity is necessary seems to me untenable. I have asked each of the top six officers of the department this question: "Do you really mean that you are unwilling to tell the public the truth about what you are doing?" None said directly: "Yes, I am unwilling," but all said that indirectly in one form or another. All have been brought up on the system of pretending full enforcement. That is the only system any of them has ever known. They assume that that system is necessary. Yet none gave a satisfactory reason in support of it. The best any could do was to say: "If parents of teenagers learn that we don't arrest for smoking marijuana, for instance, we'll be in for a bad time. We're not going to ask for unnecessary trouble." To that, my question was: "Does that mean you are opposed to letting the public influence your enforcement poli-

Ch. 3 *PRETENDED FULL ENFORCEMENT*

cies?" The answer: "We'll just have unnecessary difficulty if we create a lot of issues we don't now have." I agree that dictatorship can be more efficient than a democratic process, but I favor public participation. Parents of teenagers should have a voice in police enforcement policy about marijuana, even at the cost of some "difficulty" to the police. The false pretense effectively shuts off that voice.

**Reasons for getting rid of the false pretense.**

I cannot discuss sound reasons for *keeping* the false pretense of full enforcement, for I know of none, except that it is the product of accretions of history. The problem seems to be the rare one where all the reasons are on one side.

Five reasons against the false pretense are discussed in the first paragraph of this chapter—the false pretense prevents the top officers from making enforcement policy and requires patrolmen to be the principal makers of such policy, it prevents studies of enforcement policy, it deters employment of specialized staffs to make enforcement policy, it discourages open processes that would invite community participation and criticism, and it cuts off coordination of police enforcement policy with the policy of prosecutors and judges.

Two additional reasons against the system of false pretense, rather obvious ones, are that deliberate deception of the public by the police is morally objectionable, and that direct and purposeful violation by the police of what they believe to be the law is contrary to the heart of the fundamental principle we call "the rule of law."

Beyond those negative reasons against the system of the false pretense, I shall discuss three main affirmative reasons for full and honest disclosure of enforcement policy to the public: (1) Any public agency, because it is a public agency, should make its policies known. (2) Fairness requires that those affected have a chance to know the enforcement policies. (3) The public, in my opinion, will prefer the truth about selective enforcement to continuing the false pretense of full enforcement.

(1) All public officers at times have a tendency to assume that the agency they work for is their establishment and that what they do is their business and nobody else's. But the top officers of the Chicago police department are not the proprietors of a private business. They work for the pub-

## Ch. 3 *PRETENDED FULL ENFORCEMENT*

lic. In a democratic system, the members of the public—the electorate—are their bosses. And the bosses have a right to know what is going on.

Legislative bodies are increasingly requiring administrative openness. The Freedom of Information Act requires all federal agencies to open their records to public inspection. In state governments, a wave of "government in the sunshine" legislation is tending to cover the country, and the movement has not yet run its course. But openness of government agencies, whether or not required, has long been the policy of the best administrators. We Americans don't want dictators; we want a chance to know and a chance to criticize what our public servants are doing. Otherwise, we believe, government by bureaucrats is likely to be in the interest of the bureaucrats and not in the interest of the public.

(2) Fairness requires that those affected by law should have a chance to know what the law is. When a legislative body enacts a statute or an ordinance making an act a crime, concealment of the statute or ordinance would be outrageous, as all who are committed to our general system of government are likely to agree. Similarly, repeal of criminal legislation should also be knowa-

ble; to require one to comply with legislation that has been repealed would be unfair. So one who cannot know of the repeal would be unjustly treated.

Criminal law has two sides—the formality and the reality. The formality is found in statute books and in opinions of appellate courts. The reality is found in the practices of enforcement officers. Drinking in the park is a crime according to the ordinance, but quietly drinking at a family picnic without disturbing others is not a crime according to the reality of the law, because officers uniformly refuse to enforce the ordinance in such circumstances. When the formality and the reality differ, the reality is the one that prevails. When the officer says, "I won't interfere if you drink quietly," the words of the ordinance, the formality, are superseded by the enforcement policy, the reality.

If, then, I am right that concealing criminal statutes and ordinances from those affected would be outrageous, as well as concealing the repeal or partial repeal of statutes or ordinances, concealing the reality of the law, the enforcement policy, would be even more outrageous, because the reality is what counts.

## Ch. 3 *PRETENDED FULL ENFORCEMENT*

Of course, I do not say that enforcement strategies or allocations of police manpower must be disclosed. If extra men are assigned to a high crime area, disclosure might defeat the purpose. But when the policy is that an officer will not arrest for a crime committed in his presence, that reality of the law should be disclosed, for nonenforcement is the practical equivalent of repeal or partial repeal of the criminal legislation.

Some say that unenforced legislation may have a deterrent effect that will be destroyed by disclosure of the lack of enforcement and that therefore disclosure is undesirable. The consensual sex crimes are an example. If the police can't and don't enforce, should they nevertheless pretend to enforce and thereby induce some compliance? The question seems to be subject to difference of opinion, but I think honesty of a government agency is the best policy. I think the man and woman who want to live together without marriage should be entitled to know that, in absence of special circumstances, the police have not enforced the fornication statute for many decades.

(3) In our interviews we have learned that the Chicago police uniformly believe that the public would disapprove any nonen-

*PRETENDED FULL ENFORCEMENT* Ch. 3

forcement policy they might learn about. My opinion is that the reasons for nonenforcement are often entirely sound and that when the reasons are sound a persuasive statement of them is likely to win public approval. The public can understand the reasons for nonenforcement, including limited police resources, longterm legislative acquiescence in selective enforcement, the need for enforcement priorities, and the propriety of leniency in some circumstances.

Specific experience of the Chicago police supports my view. When Chicago policemen during the 1960s arrested a group of prominent men for playing poker at the home of one of them, Superintendent O. W. Wilson announced to the press that he was sorry and that he was giving instructions not to arrest for social gambling. The public did not rise up and say that Wilson had no authority to change the Illinois statute making gambling a crime and making no exception for social gambling. Instead, the public response was uniformly favorable. The statute remained on the books, but those who wanted to engage in social gambling were more secure. Similarly, a Chicago newspaper reported February 16, 1966: "Chicago Police Supt. Orlando W. Wilson said Tuesday that city policemen will continue to ig-

Ch. 3 *PRETENDED FULL ENFORCEMENT*

nore jaywalking. On the basis of a two-month study of cities that enforce jaywalking laws, he explained, his men will leave well enough alone. He said that Chicago's pedestrian death rate is substantially lower than in cities that have had enforcement programs for years." Wilson did not ask for repeal of the ordinance, and as of 1975 it remains on the books, unenforced. Repeal of the ordinance would no doubt have been better, but the present point is that no outcry came from the public that the Superintendent was usurping legislative power. The public accepted and still accepts the nonenforcement.

Superintendent O. W. Wilson even had the courage to say in general terms that selective enforcement is essential. In a widely circulated pamphlet entitled "On This We Stand," he said on behalf of the police department at page 2: "The police must necessarily exercise discretion in the enforcement of the laws because of the limited resources available to them . . . Enforcement must be selective to be most effective . . . It must be selective as to time and place . . . It must also be selective as to the relative importance of crimes." What he said was true when he said it and it remains true today. The public did not criticize him adversely for speaking the truth. The public today would not criticize his successors adversely if they were to substitute the truth for their false pretense.

Of course, the public may object to nonenforcement of particular statutes or ordinances. I, for one, strongly object to some of the present selective enforcement practices; I feel shocked to learn that one caught in the act of burglary may be immune from arrest because he is giving the police information about narcotics dealers. And I am shocked that the police customarily do not arrest for attempted bribery of police officers even when they have witnesses to the attempted bribery. I also believe that arrests should normally be made for serious crimes whenever witnesses are available to testify to the crime, whether or not the victim of the crime is willing to sign a complaint. Various other enforcement policies I disagree with and I think the public generally may. But that is not a reason against disclosure of those policies; instead, it is a reason *for* such disclosure. Every policy, unless confidentiality is necessary, should have to run the gauntlet of public criticism. If it does not survive, then it should not survive.

## Ch. 3 *PRETENDED FULL ENFORCEMENT*

Altogether, I think the reasons against the false pretense of full enforcement are very powerful, and that nothing stands in the way of an open policy of selective enforcement, except the police belief that such an open policy would violate the full enforcement legislation. That is the subject of the next chapter.

## CHAPTER 4

## THE LEGALITY OF OPEN SELECTIVE ENFORCEMENT

### The full enforcement legislation is clear on its face.

We saw in the last chapter that the police *cannot* enforce all criminal law, that they interpret the full enforcement legislation literally, and that the result, from which many unfortunate consequences flow, is that the police use a system of selective enforcement but falsely pretend to have a system of full enforcement. My opinion is that the false pretense is extremely damaging and stands in the way of a sound system. Complete disclosure of selective enforcement seems to me essential. Yet the full enforcement legislation set forth above in the second section of chapter 3 says that full enforcement is required.

Although I favor repeal of the full enforcement legislation and although I expect that it will be repealed sooner or later, the problem can be solved without repeal. The police in my opinion should openly acknowledge that for more than a century they have

## Ch. 4  SELECTIVENESS IS LEGAL

used a system of selective enforcement. Such a system is entirely legal, as I now shall try to show.

The starting point on the question of legality has to be the words of the full enforcement statute and ordinances. Those words unquestionably call for full enforcement. They even do so emphatically and without ambiguity. Furthermore, no legislative history to the contrary has come to light. The meaning is so plain that everyone who can read English is likely to find essentially the same meaning. Ever since the Illinois statute was enacted before 1845, the Chicago police apparently have consistently assumed that they are bound by the plain meaning, and they still so assume.

If the problem of legality had to be solved solely on the basis of the full enforcement legislation, the answer would be that full enforcement is required.

## Legislative intent expressed outside the full enforcement legislation, combined with impossibility of full enforcement.

The legislative bodies have expressed their intent in the full enforcement legislation, and they have also expressed their intent elsewhere. They have spoken with three voices. The first is the full enforcement legislation. The second is knowledge of and acquiescence in the police system of selective enforcement over a period of more than a century. Legislators know that their criminal legislation often overshoots. Their draftsmen know that if they make too much criminal, the law enforcement people—police, prosecutors, and judges—will cut it back to make it sensible. Their intent often is clear that the police should not interpret criminal legislation literally and then enforce it fully. The third voice—the most powerful of the three—is appropriation of only enough for an estimated half to two-thirds of full enforcement. The Chicago police have 13,400 people and an annual budget of $254 million. Some say full enforcement might require 26,800 people and $508 million. A better understanding, of course, is that full enforcement of present law probably could not feasibly be achieved, no matter how much the resources were increased. At all events, all informed persons are in agreement that full enforcement is impossible with the present appropriation and the present system of operation. So the legislative voice in the appropriation speaks with irresistible power; the police clearly lack the resources for full enforcement.

## Ch. 4   *SELECTIVENESS IS LEGAL*

The inconsistency is between (a) the full enforcement legislation, pulling in one direction, and (b) the longterm legislative acquiescence in selective enforcement, plus appropriation of only enough for partial enforcement, pulling in the opposite direction. That legislative inconsistency, I think, has to be resolved the way the police have in fact resolved it, because resolving it in favor of full enforcement is impossible.

Therefore, although the case for literal interpretation of the full enforcement legislation is both obvious and strong, I believe the case for non-literal interpretation, though far from obvious, is unanswerable, even though it is based on a somewhat sophisticated analysis that may have little appeal to those lawyers and judges who make quick decisions without digging below the surface.

### Four main types of enforcement problems and the case for legality of selective enforcement.

The problem of legality of selective enforcement need not be resolved the same way for all problems. Selective enforcement can be legal in some circumstances and not in others. I believe that the reasons in support of legality are sometimes conclusive, but that even when they are at their weakest they suffice.

For convenience, I shall divide enforcement problems into four main types: (1) Should the police arrest when they know the prosecutors will not prosecute or the court will dismiss? (2) Do the police violate the full enforcement legislation when a crime is committed in their presence but arrest is (a) physically impossible, (b) less important than some other urgent duty, or (c) impossible on account of limited resources? (3) Does insufficiency of police resources for full enforcement justify a system of enforcement priorities that takes into account all relevant reasons for enforcing or not enforcing, or must the police indiscriminately try to enforce on any and all occasions, so that what remains unenforced on account of limited resources will not be determined by policy reasons but by fortuities of what happens to come first? (4) Are the police always forbidden to make enforcement decisions on individualized grounds?

(1) Whether we like it or not—and whether the police like it or not—prosecutors do not prosecute for all offenses. They pick and choose, partly on the basis of protecting themselves against too much work,

## Ch. 4 SELECTIVENESS IS LEGAL

partly on the basis of their own policy preferences, partly on the basis (sometimes) of their own political advantage, and partly on the basis of conscientious appraisals of probability of a conviction. When a patrolman encounters a youth who is smoking marijuana in a public place but who possesses only the one partial stick, what should the patrolman do if he knows that the prosecutor who will handle the case will refuse to prosecute? Should he make what seems to him a futile arrest? Does the full enforcement legislation require him to? Or does the legislative body intend that arrests be made only when they are not believed to be futile? The answer does not appear on the face of the legislation, and therefore the answer has to be found by inquiring what a reasonable legislative body would have provided if it had answered the question explicitly. I think the answer is obvious. And I think the answer is the same when the patrolman knows that a judge will dismiss the case if the prosecutor brings it. This is a circumstance, I think, when no reasonable person would interpret the full enforcement legislation literally.

(2) If A and B commit a crime in a patrolman's presence and run in different directions, what does the full enforcement

legislation require the patrolman to do? Run after both? Surely he cannot be required to do what is physically impossible. Similarly, what if the patrolman is in hot pursuit of a robber when he sees someone drinking in the park? It is possible for him to arrest the drinker, and literal interpretation will require him to. Could a reasonable legislative body have intended that, especially if the patrolman thinks he has a good chance of catching the robber? The next step is to ask: If a single patrolman finds that he cannot enforce against all violators, major and minor, must he arrest every minor violator who commits a crime in his presence, at the risk of neglecting some major violators, or may he make plans to maximize his effectiveness by emphasizing serious crimes, even if the result is nonarrest for some minor crimes committed in his presence? And one more step is to ask: May the patrolman who is sensibly trying to maximize his effectiveness by neglecting some minor crimes make policy judgments not only about what is major and what is minor but also about what the community probably wants, about probable consequences of enforcement or nonenforcement, and in each instance about how to evaluate one or another course of action or inaction? The

## Ch. 4 *SELECTIVENESS IS LEGAL*

final step is to ask: If the whole police force estimates that its resources (appropriation and manpower) suffice for only from a half to two-thirds of full enforcement (as high officers do estimate, while disclaiming capacity to measure), do they violate the full enforcement legislation if they establish and follow a system of enforcement priorities that is designed to emphasize what they believe to be most important, while sacrificing what they regard as relatively unimportant?

My answer is that proper interpretation, as well as good sense, requires a system of enforcement priorities, even if the result is nonenforcement for some crimes committed in the presence of an officer.

(3) When the system of enforcement priorities is compelled by insufficient resources, the system obviously must be planned on the basis of all relevant policy reasons for and against enforcing in each instance. No reasonable legislative body could have intended that resources should be indiscriminately used up on whatever comes first, so that some of the most vital enforcement tasks would in the end remain undone for lack of resources.

(4) The fourth question, whether the police are always forbidden to make enforce-

ment decisions on individualized grounds, is the only one of the four questions about which I have any subjective doubt. If A and B have both violated in the officer's presence, may he, on individualized grounds, make a deliberate choice to enforce against A but not against B, without violating the full enforcement legislation? For instance, A, a 12-year-old, and B, a 42-year-old, have both ridden their bicycles the wrong way on a one-way street in the officer's presence. The officer accosts A, who politely says he did not know the law and won't violate again. The officer has cautioned B before, and B insolently says he thinks the law is crazy. Giving B a ticket is obviously justified. May the officer properly let A go? Will he violate the full enforcement legislation if he does no more than explain to the boy the reasons behind the law? One answer is: The words of the full enforcement legislation are clear; no exception is made for the boy in these circumstances. Is that a satisfactory answer? Did the legislature really intend that, or did it mean, even though it failed to say so, that it intended to allow the normal kind of individualizing discretion to the enforcing officer? Probably an answer either way would be reasonable, but I prefer to interpret the legislation to al-

Ch. 4   *SELECTIVENESS IS LEGAL*

low some individualizing discretion, and that is what I think nearly all good judges would do.

**The story of Patrolman X.**

One elderly patrolman we interviewed I shall call Patrolman X. With justified pride, he has told us about the relationships he has established with boys who have committed minor crimes. Often he has counseled them instead of taking them into custody—instead of doing his statutory duty "forthwith to apprehend the offender." In the cases he likes to talk about, his guidance has not only kept the boys out of trouble, but he takes great satisfaction in pointing out that four of them, now young men, are wearing police uniforms. He says they are "good cops." He thinks that punishing them for their minor crimes could have pushed them toward more serious crimes.

Patrolman X does not deny that his leniency was directly opposed to the words of the full enforcement legislation. And he makes no legal analysis in self defense. But he says he has never been disciplined for being lenient. His supervisors have been generally unaware of his leniency, but he thinks they would have approved if they had known all the facts. And he insists that every officer of the Chicago police department who is engaged in law enforcement violates the literal words of the full enforcement legislation several times a day. "Everybody knows," he says, "that you can't enforce everything." The criminal legislation is only a framework. Often it doesn't fit. What matters, he thinks, is what happens to the boys. He seems to know a good deal about normal boys and the crimes they commit. He talks about throwing rocks, other vandalism, issues with neighbors who don't like their noisy play, drinking beer, theft of a candy bar, and curfew violations. He also talks about serious crimes—gangs and gang wars, auto thefts, purse snatching, use of firearms, robberies. He does a good deal of individualizing. He is not always lenient. But he seems quite secure in his belief that sometimes he *should* be.

Is he wrong in that belief? Should the literal words be applied to him? Should he always take a boy to the youth officer, even if he thinks he can better handle the case himself, or even if he knows that taking the boy to the youth officer will be a waste of time because that officer will immediately release the boy? If the legislators who more than a century ago enacted the Illinois full enforcement statute were to hear the story

## Ch. 4  *SELECTIVENESS IS LEGAL*

of Patrolman X, and if they were then to be explicit about their intent, as they have not been except in very broad terms, what would they say? Would they condemn him for violating their cryptic words? Or would they congratulate him on the fact of which he is most proud—that four of his "boys" now wear police uniforms instead of jail uniforms?

Of course, not many patrolmen have had Patrolman X's successes in dealing with minor violators, and perhaps some patrolmen should not be trusted with such discretionary power. But the answer to that observation is not in the literal words of the full enforcement legislation; the answer is in carefully-prepared rules to guide patrolmen and in proper supervision of patrolmen, and that is what I propose in chapters 5 and 6. The point I make now is that adherence to the literal terms of the full enforcement legislation would produce unwanted results.

### May a police rule legally provide for nonenforcement of a criminal statute or ordinance?

My answer is yes, but the answer of almost all police officers who have no legal training is no, and therefore the question calls for discussion.

*SELECTIVENESS IS LEGAL* Ch. 4

This question arises even apart from the full enforcement legislation. The heart of the question that troubles police officers is whether the police may through nonenforcement cut back a criminal statute enacted by a legislative body. The question can be better understood through a specific illustration. The Illinois Criminal Code, ch. 38, § 11–8, provides a fine up to $200 and imprisonment up to six months for fornication: "Any person who cohabits or has sexual intercourse with another not his spouse commits fornication if the behavior is open and notorious." Let us assume a hypothetical rule that the police ordinarily will not arrest a man and a woman who openly live together without marriage, in absence of special circumstances. Let us assume hypothetical facts that two graduate students, a man and a woman, both 24, live together on or near a university campus, and that their cohabitation is "open and notorious" in that their friends and acquaintances know that they live together and that they are not married. They clearly violate the words of the statute, but they are clearly within the rule because of "absence of special circumstances." Is the rule as thus applied legal?

The police generally say no. The legislature has made the cohabitation a crime.

## Ch. 4  SELECTIVENESS IS LEGAL

Therefore the police cannot make it not a crime. The police are a subordinate agency, having no power to undo what the legislative body does. Accordingly, the police usually say, a rule that the police do not enforce must be invalid. Almost every police officer seems instinctively to accept this argument. All his training and all his experience support his instinct. His job is to enforce the law, not to change the law. He has always understood that he has to carry out what the legislature enacts.

The police usually *say* that a nonenforcement rule would be illegal. But they do in fact have a consistent practice of not enforcing the statute when the facts are as assumed. So we have four questions: (1) Is nonenforcement legal? (2) May the police legally follow a consistent practice of nonenforcement? (3) Is a consistent practice an unwritten rule? (4) If an unwritten rule is legal, would a written rule to the same effect be legal?

If (1) the answer to the first question is yes, as police action says it is and as I say it is, then the answers to the other questions have to be (2) that a legal practice may be legally followed consistently, (3) that any administrator's consistent practice may properly be called an unwritten rule, and (4) that if an unwritten rule is legal a written rule to the same effect has to be legal.

The police argument for invalidity of a rule that prescribes nonenforcement is based on a theory of how our institutions are supposed to work, not on the reality of the way they do in fact work. The plain reality is that from the beginning of American government, a gap has existed between statutory law and enforced law. When legislative bodies learn that enforcement officers are enforcing something less than the enacted law, they seldom legislate to insist that the enacted law be enforced, as they are entitled to do if they want to; instead, they generally express their appreciation to the enforcement agencies for contributing to a sensible system. Almost all legislators are fully aware that the system would not be sensible if every criminal statute were enforced according to its letter.

For more than a century all American legislative bodies that enact criminal statutes have had a basic intent without expressing it directly: They intend that enforcement officers should cut back enacted criminal law to what is enforceable, to what is sensible, and to what the community wants and expects.

## Ch. 4  SELECTIVENESS IS LEGAL

That is the reality even though it is not the theory.

Instead of the system we have, I would much prefer a system in which the theory and the reality would coincide, a system in which the legislatures would make careful inquiries into what can or cannot be enforced and tailor their statutes accordingly, a system in which the statutes would be formulated so that full enforcement would be sensible and would provide what the community wants, a system in which police nonenforcement of a statute would be illegal, and a system in which a rule providing for nonenforcement would be illegal.

But that is not our system. It never has been.

If we answer the question of legality on the basis of the reality of what our system is in fact, and not on the basis of some theory that is contrary to the reality, our conclusion has to be that a police nonenforcement rule is entirely legal.

The International Association of Chiefs of Police, in a set of Model Rules based on Texas law, specifically provides that an officer may "decline to arrest notwithstanding existence of probable cause to arrest," despite a Texas full enforcement statute. I agree with the Association. (See the discussion of the Model Rules in the second section of chapter 5.)

Of course, a legislative body is not without power to provide for full enforcement of a particular statute or ordinance, and if it makes its intent clear, its general acquiescence in nonenforcement and its appropriation of less than enough for full enforcement may be overridden by the more specific intent. Examples of special Illinois statutes calling for enforcement of particular provisions include ch. 95½, §§ 312–1 and 602–1; ch. 57½, § 78; ch. 38, § 13–4(a); whether or not these special statutes will be interpreted to have a different meaning from the more general statutes to the same effect I do not know.

**Some conclusions.**

The legislative bodies have spoken with three voices about full enforcement, and the second and third voices say the opposite of what the first says. The police say they hear only the first voice, and that is why they pretend that their system is one of full enforcement. I think the true legislative intent is expressed by the second and third voices. The second voice says that the legislative bodies know that criminal legislation

Ch. 4  *SELECTIVENESS IS LEGAL*

is excessive and that they want the police to cut it back. The second voice alone is probably enough to override the first, but the third is the loudest one, for it allows only enough appropriation for half to two-thirds of full enforcement. So I have no difficulty in concluding that selective enforcement is legal, that some nonenforcement is unavoidable, that officers should not arrest when prosecutors will not prosecute or judges will dismiss, that a system of enforcement priorities is necessary, and that the priorities may properly rest on policy considerations having no immediate relation to limited resources.

The odd fact is that the police say they hear only the first voice. That is why they pretend to enforce fully. They pretend in the formal rules and regulations of the police board, they pretend in their general and special orders, they pretend when they avoid any statement from a superior to a subordinate directing nonenforcement, and they pretend to us in our interviews.

The false pretense has prevented the police department from growing into a natural and healthy organization. It is stunted and deformed. Its high officers usually assume that they cannot make enforcement policy, cannot make studies of what the policy should be, cannot get assistance from profes-

[96]

sional staffs, and cannot coordinate their enforcement policy with other organs of government. The false pretense—the deformity—has prevented the police from developing in the way that other governmental organizations in this country normally do.

The deformity can be corrected. A surgical operation can remove the false pretense that has retarded the development. Then the organization can grow in the normal fashion. It can tell the truth about its enforcement policy. It can say openly and proudly that its system is one of selective enforcement. And it can then take all the action that has been held back all these years by the unfortunate deformity. It then can grow in ways that other governmental organizations have grown, including ways that are proposed in chapters 5 and 6.

## CHAPTER 5

## RULES AND RULEMAKING PROCEDURE

**The need for rules.**

The police obviously need rules. That is why they have always had rules, such as the present general orders and special orders. Running a department of 13,400 people can hardly be done without some sort of rules. The question worth raising is whether rules to govern or to guide enforcement policy are desirable. I think they are. Indeed, the only reason the department does not now have such rules is that such rules would be incompatible with the false pretense that the only enforcement policy is one of full enforcement. As soon as the department understands with sufficient clarity that an open policy that includes some nonenforcement and some partial enforcement is not illegal, I think it will quite naturally develop enforcement policy through rules. That seems to me inevitable, the only question being whether the development will come sooner or whether it will come later.

Too many present enforcement policies vary with the whims of particular officers.

*RULES AND RULEMAKING* Ch. 5

As I try to show in chapter 7, patrolmen should have discretion to do the necessary individualizing in the light of all facts and circumstances of particular cases, but they should in general be denied discretionary power to determine an overall policy in a particular case. The Chicago police are seriously deficient, in my opinion, in the extent to which disparity from case to case produces a denial of equal justice. Rules to guide and to govern the overall policy in each case are an obvious tool for a better system of police justice.

Not only do the Chicago police need enforcement rules but they also need the benefits that will flow from making enforcement policy through rulemaking procedure. In the rest of this chapter, I shall discuss the movement toward police rulemaking, rulemaking procedure, police authority to make rules, and the newly developing law about judicially required rulemaking. Then at the end of the chapter is one of the most important sections in this book—a statement of fourteen reasons in favor of police rulemaking on the subject of selective enforcement.

## The movement toward police rulemaking.

The President's Crime Commission recommended in 1967: "Police departments should

Ch. 5  *RULES AND RULEMAKING*

develop and enunciate policies that give police personnel specific guidance for the common situations requiring exercise of police discretion," after pointing out that the customary police manuals "almost never discuss . . . the hard choices policemen must make every day." The Challenge of Crime in a Free Society 103–04. The Commission said nothing of rulemaking procedure. In my 1969 book on Discretionary Justice, pages 90–91, I wrote a section entitled "What rule-making procedure can accomplish for police policy," stating ten objectives of a good program for reform of police practices, and strongly advocating rulemaking procedure. My view is that having a set of rules is not enough. What is also needed is the right procedure for developing the rules. My recommendation has been picked up and furthered by three important organizations.

The American Bar Association's Project on Standards for Criminal Justice published in 1973 its final draft of Standards Relating to the Urban Police Function. Standard 4.3 asserts: "Police discretion can best be structured and controlled through the process of administrative rule-making by police agencies. Police administrators should, therefore, give the highest priority to the formulation of administrative rules governing the exercise of discretion, particularly in the areas of selective enforcement, investigative techniques, and enforcement methods." Note the emphasis on "the process." The standards were unanimously adopted by the American Bar Association's House of Delegates.

The National Advisory Commission on Criminal Justice Standards and Goals, appointed by the Law Enforcement Assistance Administration, in its 1973 report on Police recommended at page 21 in Standard 1.3 that every police agency should adopt "comprehensive policy statements that publicly establish the limits of discretion, that provide guidelines for its exercise within those limits, and that eliminate discriminatory enforcement of the law. . . . Every police chief executive should establish policy that guides the exercise of discretion by police personnel in using arrest alternatives. . . . Every police chief executive should formalize procedures for developing and implementing the foregoing written agency policy." The last sentence focuses on "procedures."

The International Association of Chiefs of Police has not only approved the ABA Standards on the Urban Police Function by

## Ch. 5  RULES AND RULEMAKING

a unanimous vote of its Executive Committee but it has gone further than any other organization in that it has sponsored the preparation of a set of Model Rules for Law Enforcement Officers. The Model Rules were prepared by the Criminal Justice Council of Texas and are based on Texas law. Along with the commentary on the rules, they fill 289 pages and deal with nine subjects: Domestic Disturbances, Misdemeanor Field Release by Citation, Use of Force, Fresh Pursuit, Rules for Arrest Without a Warrant, Warrantless Search and Seizure, Execution of Arrest Warrants, Execution of Search Warrants, and Stop-And-Frisk.

The movement toward police rulemaking is still in its early stages, and it is rapidly gaining momentum. A good many model rules have been prepared by Arizona State University's Project on Law Enforcement Policy and Rule-Making. None of the rules drafted so far have tackled the difficult subject of selective enforcement, but that should come at an early time, after experience has been gained on less difficult subjects. The Model Rules for Texas do recognize selective enforcement. In chapter 5, § 6.01 provides at page 176: "An officer is not obliged to make an arrest in every instance. He may in some circumstances, for good cause consistent with the public interest, decline to arrest notwithstanding the existence of probable cause to arrest." Then it lists seven factors for the officer to consider. The provision of § 6.10, in my opinion, is precisely what is needed: "Where it has been determined that certain criminal laws shall not be enforced, the officer shall not arrest for those offenses. This determination should be made only through an established departmental administrative rulemaking procedure which provides for citizen participation and judicial review."

The IACP recommends that provision for Texas, even though Texas has a full enforcement statute in C.C.P. art. 2.13, which requires an officer to make an arrest whenever he is authorized to. The comment on the Model Rules says that "full enforcement of all laws, regardless of its desirability, is impossible. . . . Section 6.10 recommends that a police department formulate and promulgate policies concerning whether or not arrests should be made in specific situations involving specific offenses."

**Rulemaking procedure.**

So far as I know, rulemaking procedure is completely unknown to American police. Neither in the literature nor in my consulta-

## Ch. 5 RULES AND RULEMAKING

tions with police officers have I found any trace of any police procedure resembling the rulemaking procedure that is tried and tested in federal administrative agencies. That procedure long predated its adoption into the Administrative Procedure Act in 1946. Under the APA, that procedure has flourished. It has become a mainstay of federal governmental processes. And during the last three or four years, we have had a veritable explosion of rulemaking activity within the federal government. My guess is that rulemaking will continue to surge upwards. It will become the principal way by which administrative policy is worked out. It will be the main method for filling in the statutes enacted by Congress—statutes that go about as far as congressmen are capable of going but which leave a very great deal of policymaking for administrators to work out. Policymaking through the forms of adjudication rose to a peak during the past three decades, but it is declining, and I predict that it will continue to decline. Rulemaking procedure is vastly superior for most policymaking. The procedure of adjudication will be more and more confined to resolving issues of specific fact; it will be used less and less for resolving questions of policy and questions of broad or general fact.

The rulemaking procedure that is marked out by the Administrative Procedure Act, 5 U.S.C. § 553, is commonly called notice-and-comment procedure. The agency makes its studies, perhaps consults some affected parties informally, and prepares proposed rules. The essence of the procedure is the publication of the proposed rules in the Federal Register, along with invitations for written comments. The key statutory words are those of § 553(c): "After notice required by this section, the agency shall give interested persons an opportunity to participate in the rule making through submission of written data, views, or arguments with or without opportunity for oral presentation. After consideration of the relevant matter presented, the agency shall incorporate in the rules adopted a concise general statement of their basis and purpose." Usually no oral process, except that of informal conversations, is used, but occasionally argument-type hearings are held. Usually the agency simply receives whatever written materials interested parties care to submit, has its staff sift and summarize the materials, and makes such revisions in the proposed rules as it sees fit. Then it publishes the final rules, along with the "concise general statement of their basis

## Ch. 5  RULES AND RULEMAKING

and purpose." Anyone may apply to the agency for changes in the rules at any time.

The procedure is highly efficient. Everyone has a chance to submit whatever he wants to submit—studies, data, opinions, arguments, analyses, statistics, experience, preferences, emotions. Even when the studies that produced the proposed rules have been very thorough, a typical agency usually learns a good deal from the written submissions, especially about the probable impact of the proposed rules on particular parties. The time consumed by the procedure is minimal.

The procedure is democratic. Those affected have a chance to express their preferences and to submit their arguments. Those affected especially have a chance to tell the agency how the proposed rules will affect them and to make suggestions—often suggestions that are helpful to the agency—as to how to modify the proposed rules in order to accomplish their purpose without unnecessarily hurting particular parties.

Clearly the police should learn about notice-and-comment rulemaking procedure, and clearly they should experiment with it. Yet I realize that the background of the police, their habits, and their attitudes seem to lead them away from such procedure. At a meeting of a hundred Texas police administrators in April, 1974, Captain Robert Allen of the San Antonio police, an individual far ahead of most of his colleagues, was advocating police rules, and he carried his audience with him in expressing embarrassment when rules that he drafted leaked out to the press while they were still tentative. To my question of why he had not systematically planned to give the tentative rules to the press, he expressed astonishment—and he still had his audience with him: "We don't want the press to publish our thinking until we've made up our minds. We'll publish our rules when we get them finished, but not before then."

I think Captain Allen deserves commendation for police leadership in rulemaking, and I predict that in time he will see the advantages of publishing tentative rules as an effective means of trying to perfect them. The police, I think, can learn from the vast experience of federal agencies.

### Police authority to make rules.

Statutes do not customarily confer rulemaking power upon the police. No Illinois statute or Chicago ordinance does. In absence of a grant of rulemaking power, may

## Ch. 5  RULES AND RULEMAKING

the Chicago police make rules? If making rules involves an exercise of legislative power, and if no such legislative power has been delegated to the police, how can they legislate through rulemaking? Furthermore, if a legislative body even when it does delegate legislative power must lay down meaningful standards or run afoul of the constitutional nondelegation doctrine, and if no such standards to guide police rulemaking have ever been developed, how could police rules be constitutional?

The rather clear answer to this cluster of questions is, in my opinion, that the police have a rulemaking power, and that rules they might make on enforcement policy could be legal and constitutional, but the rules would not necessarily have the force of law.

On the question of possible lack of authority, we turn to Supreme Court law. When Congress created the Wage-Hour Administration in 1938, it debated the question whether to confer a rulemaking power upon it, and decided not to. But the Wage-Hour Administration was assigned the duty of enforcing the legislation, and it systematically stated its enforcement policies in periodic Interpretative Bulletins, now gathered together in the Code of Federal Regulations.

*RULES AND RULEMAKING* Ch. 5

When a problem of applying the statute came to the Supreme Court in Skidmore v. Swift & Co., 323 U.S. 134 (1944), the Court followed the Interpretative Bulletin, declaring that the Administrator's interpretations, "while not controlling upon the courts by reason of their authority, do constitute a body of experience and informed judgment to which courts and litigants may properly resort for guidance." The Court called the rules "interpretative regulations."

The case for police rulemaking is even stronger than the case for rulemaking by the Wage-Hour Administration, for no legislative body has debated the question whether to confer a rulemaking power upon the police and then decided not to. The question of rulemaking power of the police has not been debated by a legislative body. So if a rulemaking power exists even when the legislative body has specifically withheld it, as the unanimous Supreme Court held in the Skidmore case, it must exist when the legislative body has not considered the question whether the enforcing agency should have a rulemaking power.

The principle of the Skidmore case is a fundamental one, I think. It is that any agency which has discretionary power necessarily has the power to state publicly the

## Ch. 5  *RULES AND RULEMAKING*

manner in which the agency will exercise the power. Such a public statement can be adopted through a rulemaking procedure, whether or not the legislative body has separately conferred a rulemaking power on the agency.

Such rules as are adopted in absence of a grant of legislative power to make rules are regarded as interpretative rules and do not necessarily have force of law. So-called "legislative rules" that have force of law, like statutes, cannot be validly issued in absence of a legislative grant of power to make rules having force of law. For the purpose to be served by police rules governing or guiding enforcement policies, interpretative rules will be at least as satisfactory as legislative rules, and they might sometimes be better in that they will not necessarily be controlling in suits that seek to impose tort liability on police officers.

Quite independently of the Skidmore doctrine, the legality of police rulemaking may be established. Any executive, such as a superintendent of police, may give instructions to his subordinates, may call the instructions rules, may open them to public inspection, and in preparing them may follow appropriate rulemaking procedure. The courts are then free, as in Skidmore, to regard the superintendent's rules as "a body of experience and informed judgment to which courts and litigants may properly resort for guidance." The present general orders and special orders of the Chicago police are largely in the nature of rules, and they can be expanded to cover enforcement policy.

But what of the nondelegation doctrine's requirement of statutory standards; in light of that requirement how can the courts allow the police to make rules without statutory standards? The answer is a legal anomaly, a serious flaw in judicial doctrine. As I have written heretofore, "The non-delegation doctrine seems crazily incongruous when placed alongside realities of the commonplace power of selective enforcement, as exercised by police, prosecutors, regulatory agencies, and other administrators." Discretionary Justice: A Preliminary Inquiry, page 218 (1969). Selective enforcement need not be guided by standards even though it is typically exercised in individual cases, whereas making rules of general applicability is required to be guided by standards even though the dangers to justice are much less than in the decision of individual cases. The incongruity is so striking that both parts of judicial doctrine will have to move

## Ch. 5  RULES AND RULEMAKING

toward a middle position: The Courts will no longer require statutory standards but will be satisfied with administrative standards, that is, standards created by the administrators; and the courts will no longer leave selective enforcement completely uncontrolled but will gradually subject it to a judicial requirement of rules or standards to guide it in individual cases. A recent sample of judicial relinquishment of the requirement of *statutory* standards as long as the *administrative* standards are adequate is People v. Fields, 391 Mich. 206, 216 N.W.2d 51 (1974). The Fields case is one of two dozen recent decisions that seem to me to be forerunners of general law to the same effect. Five years ago I would have called such a holding a harbinger of future law. Today I think I might say that it is the law everywhere except for the fact that most judges of most courts do not yet know that that is what they are going to hold when the problem comes to them.

## Reasons for rulemaking on selective enforcement.

The reasons in favor of police rulemaking to guide and to govern selective enforcement seem to me overwhelming. I shall now summarize fourteen separate reasons. Many single items may be enough without the others. The fourteen in combination seem to me exceedingly powerful.

1. The quality of enforcement policy will be improved because it will be made by top officers instead of by patrolmen. The top officers obviously have skills and broad understanding that patrolmen typically lack. Under the present system the high officers seldom participate in making enforcement policy and are often uninformed of what it is. But whatever rulemaking is done is likely to be done by high officers. Indeed, when sharp issues attract wide public attention, the city council may inevitably take over some of the policymaking, and in some instances the Illinois legislature may. And that will be as it should be.

2. The quality of enforcement policy will be improved because the preparation of rules will lead to appropriate investigations and studies by qualified personnel, including specialists with suitable professional training. No longer will it be made primarily by the offhand guesswork of patrolmen.

3. The quality of enforcement policy will be improved because it will be made by officers who are addressing their minds to the problems of what the policies should be and

Ch. 5  *RULES AND RULEMAKING*

why. No longer will the explanation for enforcing a statute be: "Because we are required to enforce the law." No longer will the explanation for not enforcing a statute be: "Because we can't enforce everything."

4. The quality of enforcement policy will be improved by openness, for the police will further develop those practices that the public approves and will minimize or eliminate those that cannot stand the light of day. The story of Patrolman X above in chapter 4 is an example of what will be likely to receive encouragement. Practices at the other end of the spectrum may often have to be discontinued, such as some involving police harassment, nonarrest for serious felonies when the victim does not sign the complaint, nonarrest for attempted bribery, and deliberate destruction or confiscation of property without due process of law. Putting all law enforcement policy through the wringer of rulemaking procedure is likely to mean the elimination of numerous undesirable practices.

5. The quality of enforcement policy will be improved by suggestions and criticisms that come from the public. Even the best of administrators in federal agencies usually find that written comments on proposed

rules call to their attention effects that even the most careful studies have failed to uncover.

6. Policy formulated through rulemaking procedure is more likely to carry out community desires. Today the police usually make guesses about what the public wants. Much of the present police policy runs counter to the literal meaning of statutes enacted by the people's representatives, and secret determinations are therefore not only undemocratic but antidemocratic. Rulemaking may also lead to opinion sampling by scientific methods developed by sociologists.

7. A great gain from use of rulemaking procedure will be the education of the public in the reality that the police make vital policy. The public are now inclined to assume, as even the police do much of the time, that the police merely enforce the law and have little or nothing to do with policymaking. One reason that the police are so primitive in the methods they use for making policy is that police, legislators, and the public all tend to go along with the false pretense that all criminal law is fully enforced. What all the consequences may be of public education in the realities probably cannot be foreseen. But anyone who believes in the democratic

Ch. 5  *RULES AND RULEMAKING*

process should be pleased at the prospect of a sounder public understanding.

8. Bringing enforcement policy out into the open will increase the fairness to those affected by the policy. Fairness requires opportunity to know not only the formality of the law (statutes and judicial opinions) but also the reality of the law (what is enforced). When excessive criminal statutes are cut back by nonenforcement, one who wants to act contrary to the statute but in accordance with what the enforcement policy permits should be entitled to know the enforcement policy. A man and woman who want to live together without marriage should be entitled to know that the statute against fornication has not been enforced in such circumstances for many decades. A group of retired people who want to play cards for small stakes in the park on a summer day, with coins on the table, should be entitled to know how the police enforcement policy applies to them.

9. Open rulemaking based on the realities of the policy problems that confront the police should demonstrate to legislative bodies the need for reworking criminal legislation to bring it into accord with what is practicable from the standpoint of enforcement. When a statute makes criminal any

act from A to Z and the police enforcement policy reaches acts from A to D and is unclear about acts from E to H, what is needed is a statutory closing of the gap either from D to Z or from H to Z, or at least a narrowing of it, either by a clear direction to the police to enlarge the area of enforcement or by cutting back the statute, or by a little of each. Legislative bodies are often deficient in taking care of such problems. Open police rulemaking will either prod them or do the job for them.

10. Police rulemaking can and should gradually take the place of the somewhat unsatisfactory exclusionary rule, elaborately fabricated by the courts, now governing two or three percent of police activities. The exclusionary rule sometimes has the undesirable effect of allowing a guilty person to go free. Rules made by the police and carried out by the police can accomplish the basic purpose, without that undesirable effect.

11. Police rulemaking can gradually ease the judicial burden of fabricating and administering the exclusionary rule, a task the federal courts should never have undertaken. A better way for the federal courts to get the results the Constitution requires is to require the police to make the rules, and then

## Ch. 5  RULES AND RULEMAKING

for the courts to review the police rules. The judges can keep their fingers on the controls while at the same time shifting most of the affirmative burden of rulemaking to the police. And the judicially required rulemaking can reach all police activities, not just the two or three percent reached by the exclusionary rule. (Judicially required rulemaking is the subject of chapter 6.)

12. Police rulemaking will mean that police enforcement policy will no longer be almost completely exempt from judicial control, as it has been from the beginning of American government. A limited judicial review of the kind that is customary with respect to other administrative action is clearly desirable. Members of the bar are likely to be almost unanimous in that judgment. No one ever planned the system of unreviewability of police enforcement policy, and no one would; it just grew that way, and it stayed that way because of the combination of inertia with the inability of anyone to invent a feasible way to get away from the unreviewability. Police rules, as such, can be reviewable even before the police carry them out in any particular case, in the same way that the Supreme Court allowed preenforcement challenge of Food and Drug

Administration rules in Abbott Laboratories v. Gardner, 387 U.S. 136 (1967).

13. Open rulemaking will promote equal justice by reducing policy differences from one officer to another. The present system of allowing most enforcement policy to be made by the patrolman handling each case causes unnecessary disparity. One who is arrested for an act for which most officers do not arrest may be the victim of unfair discrimination. An enforcement policy which is always precisely equal may be unattainable, but the present disparity is wholly unnecessary and should be corrected by rules that will either direct the officer or guide his discretion.

14. Possibly most important of all is the idea that rulemaking can reduce injustice by cutting out unnecessary discretion, which is one of the prime sources of injustice. Necessary discretion must be preserved, including especially the needed individualizing—the adapting of rules to the unique facts of each case. Officers should not have power to determine in each case in accordance with their momentary whims what overall policy they prefer. They have that power now, and that is the power that rulemaking should subtract. This final reason in favor

## Ch. 5  *RULES AND RULEMAKING*

of rulemaking on selective enforcement policy is such a vital one that it is the subject of chapter 7. But first we consider in chapter 6 the important question whether courts should require police rulemaking.

## CHAPTER 6

## SHOULD COURTS REQUIRE POLICE RULEMAKING?

### Some recent administrative law.

The idea of judicially required rulemaking is a very recent one. When I advocated the idea in my 1969 book on Discretionary Justice, I had very little judicial authority in support of my position. The Supreme Court had said in 1947 that: "The function of filling in the interstices of the Act should be performed, as much as possible, through this quasi-legislative promulgation of rules . . . " SEC v. Chenery Corp., 332 U.S. 194, 202 (1947). That remark was not further developed in Supreme Court opinions, and it was overshadowed by a remark in the same opinion with an opposite thrust: "And the choice made by proceeding by general rule or by individual, ad hoc litigation is one that lies primarily in the informed discretion of the administrative agency." Id. at 203. The best case in support of my 1969 position was Holmes v. New York City Housing Authority, 398 F.2d 262 (2d Cir. 1968). The Housing Authority had 90,000 applications annually but only about 10,000 houses, and

[121]

Ch. 6  *REQUIRED POLICE RULEMAKING*

it had no systematic way of determining which applicants should get the houses. The court held that "due process requires that selections among applicants be made in accordance with 'ascertainable standards.'" Id. at 265. I interpret that to be a true fundamental: Any administrator with unguided discretionary power violates due process if he fails to confine and structure his discretion to the extent required to avoid unnecessary arbitrariness in the choices made. The decision, so interpreted, would mean that the police would be judicially required to do as much as feasible to guide enforcement through rules.

As of late 1974 about two dozen cases have further developed the same basic idea, and the body of case law is rapidly growing. Judicially required administrative rulemaking is turning out to be a highly successful tool for judicial control of administrative action in many contexts. The signs are that it will continue to blossom in many contexts. (See the partial collection of cases in my article on An Approach to Legal Control of the Police, 52 Tex.L.Rev. 703, 711 n. 16 (1974).)

An especially instructive case is Environmental Defense Fund, Inc. v. Ruckelshaus,

439 F.2d 584 (D.C.Cir. 1971). The administrator had refused to suspend the registration of DDT as a pesticide. Although the administrator clearly had discretionary power to refuse, he had not given reasons for his refusal and he had issued no rules to guide decisions about suspension. The court held that "he has an obligation to articulate the criteria that he develops in making each individual decision" and that "the task of formulating standards must not be abandoned now. . . . Courts should require administrative officers to articulate the standards and principles that govern their discretionary decisions in as much detail as possible. Rules and regulations should be freely formulated by administrators, and revised when necessary." Id. at 596, 598.

As applied to the police, the case could mean that in arresting or not arresting, the police must "articulate the criteria" that guide each decision. That would be done through rules or guidelines that state "the standards and principles." In other words, the court would require police rulemaking.

The 1974 decision of the Supreme Court of the United States in Morton v. Ruiz, 415 U.S. 199 (1974), is an important decision involving judicially required rulemaking. Ruiz, an Indian living near a reservation, brought a class action against the Secretary of the Interior claiming entitlement to public assistance benefits. The Bureau of Indian Affairs denied benefits in a letter to Ruiz, explaining that the Indian Affairs Manual limited eligibility to Indians living "on" a reservation or living in Alaska or Oklahoma. The Supreme Court first rejected the Secretary's argument that Congress intended to exclude Indians living "near" a reservation, but said that the Secretary was not necessarily without power to "allocate the limited funds" in accordance with "reasonable classifications." Then the Court said that, assuming arguendo that the Secretary could limit benefits to those "on" the reservation, "the question that remains is whether this has been validly accomplished." In holding that it had not been, the Court laid down a principle of broad applicability: "[T]he agency must, at a minimum, let the standard be generally known so as to assure that it is being applied consistently and so as to avoid both the reality and the appearance of arbitrary denial of benefits to potential beneficiaries."

The requirement that the agency must "let the standard be generally known" can easily be applied to particular questions of police enforcement policy. Standards that guide officers who make and do not make arrests must be "applied consistently" and must "avoid both the reality and the appearance of arbitrary denial" of leniency. (For a criticism of other aspects of the Ruiz opinion, see K. Davis, Administrative Law Surprises in the Ruiz Case, 75 Col.L.Rev. —— (1975).)

## The extra-judicial positions of Judges McGowan and Wright.

Two leading federal judges have freely expressed their views in legal periodicals about judicially required rulemaking, and their leadership seems likely to be followed. Both are judges of the Court of Appeals for the District of Columbia.

The article by Judge Carl McGowan is Rule-Making and the Police, 70 Mich.L.Rev. 659 (1972). The main thesis is that police rulemaking should be considered as an alternative to the exclusionary rule. Judge McGowan says: "The making of rules externally for police conduct suffers from two principal limitations. One is the absence of direct police involvement in the process. The other is the question of appropriate sanctions to assure their enforcement. The two obviously interact upon each other." He says that "greater participation by the police in the making of rules for their own guidance . . . embraces the prospect not only of progressively higher elevations in the quality of police performance, but also of relieving the courts of the necessity of seeming to obscure the search for truth by rejecting reliable evidence." He emphasizes the potentiality of judicial review of the rules: "The last word as to the propriety of police-made rules always remains with the judicial branch." Although he says that the question whether courts could require police rulemaking is "presently unresolvable," he pulls strongly in the direction of such a requirement, and much of the law imposing the requirement has developed since the time he did his writing.

Judge McGowan's article is especially valuable in bringing out the link between the exclusionary rule and police rulemaking. Such rulemaking is promising as a substitute for the exclusionary rule, which sometimes requires the release of one who can be proved to be guilty. The exclusionary rule is also unsatisfactory in that its fabrication and administration consume an inordinate amount of judicial time and energy; review of and enforcement of police-made rules would be much less demanding, for the main affirmative burden of formulating the rules

*REQUIRED POLICE RULEMAKING* Ch. 6

would be on police shoulders. Of course, the greatest advantage of required police rulemaking over the exclusionary rule is that the exclusionary rule reaches only two or three percent of police activities, whereas required police rulemaking can reach almost all police activities.

Judge J. Skelly Wright has written a piece entitled Beyond Discretionary Justice, 81 Yale L.J. 575–597 (1972), reviewing my book on Discretionary Justice. He starts with strong approval of the idea that the chief hope for confining discretionary power lies in much more extensive administrative rulemaking. The piece, however, is not merely one of approving or disapproving someone else's ideas; it is highly creative. On the crucial subject of judicially required rulemaking, Judge Wright takes his own independent position, and it is independent because he seems to have missed pages 57–59 of the book, elaborating an italicized proposition that the courts should impose "*a requirement that administrators must strive to do as much as they reasonably can do to develop and to make known the needed confinements of discretionary power through standards, principles, and rules.*" Despite those pages, he sees the book as calling for "voluntary agency rule-making," and then he goes

## Ch. 6  *REQUIRED POLICE RULEMAKING*

on to present his own strong advocacy of "a reassertion of congressional power," a strengthening of the nondelegation doctrine, and, above all, recognition of "a due process right to have one's conduct governed by rules which are stated in advance" at least in some circumstances. His central idea seems to be: "Thus, in a proper circumstance, it is clearly within the power of a reviewing court to insist as a matter of constitutional law that the agency state prospective rules and standards before its decision be enforced." He also asserts without qualification that "when an agency handles a recurring problem on an ad hoc basis despite the fact that a normative standard could easily be devised, courts can and should require rule-making on the basis of their inherent supervisory powers."

That Judge Wright intended his abstract observations to apply to both police and prosecutors is shown by this especially significant passage:

> Indeed, even in the area of criminal law, where the necessity for prospective rules is most widely recognized, police, prosecutors, judges, and parole officers continue to arrest and incarcerate people on the basis of standards which are apparent only to themselves. Under a

criminal justice system which makes such conduct as petty gambling, possession of marijuana, statutory rape, and abortion criminal offenses, a large proportion of the population becomes criminal. When the law enforcement establishment picks and chooses on an ad hoc basis which of these 'criminals' are to be arrested and prosecuted, they are in effect making up the criminal law as they go along, in a manner which suits the whims and prejudices of individual policemen and prosecutors. . . . There is simply no reason why we should go on pretending this sort of ex post facto lawmaking by administrative fiat is constitutional. . . . As argued above, one element of a lawfully made decision is that it accords with previously stated and clearly articulated rules.

I predict that what Judge Wright saw so clearly in 1972 will by 1982 be seen quite clearly by most judges. Judicially required rulemaking is destined to become a mainstay of the law.

### Cases requiring police rulemaking.

Already, the newly-developed doctrine that courts may require administrative rule-

## Ch. 6 REQUIRED POLICE RULEMAKING

making has been specifically applied to the police in several cases. Judge Wright wrote the opinion in United States v. Bryant, 439 F.2d 642 (D.C.Cir. 1971), requiring the District of Columbia police to formulate administrative rules involving record keeping. The court in note 22 spoke of "an incipient but powerful trend in the law . . . a new judicial willingness to require promulgation of and obedience to rules by administrative agencies."

In Quad-City Community News Service, Inc. v. Jebens, 334 F.Supp. 8 (S.D.Iowa, 1971), a news agency sued the mayor, chief of police, and city attorney for injunction and damages for denial of press passes by the police department. The court in an elaborate opinion held: "Regulation in the area of free expression can only be tolerated when a public official's discretion is guided by narrow and specific standards which advance a compelling state interest. . . . Whatever standard Defendants employ to license journalists who are to be admitted to sites of newsworthy events must be narrowly drawn, reasonable and definite and they must be publicly available."

Quite inspiring is a 32-page opinion requiring the Philadelphia police "to formulate and submit to this Court for approval, a comprehensive program for dealing adequately with civilian complaints alleging police misconduct. It is suggested that the following guidelines should be carefully considered in such formulation: . . . Appropriate revision of police manuals and rules of procedure spelling out in some detail, in simple language, the 'do's and don'ts' of permissible conduct in dealing with civilians (for example, manifestations of racial bias, derogatory remarks, offensive language, etc.; unnecessary damage to property and other unreasonable conduct in executing search warrants; limitations on pursuit of persons charged with summary offenses; recording and processing of civilian complaints, etc.). . . . " Council of Organizations on Philadelphia Police Accountability and Responsibility v. Rizzo, 357 F.Supp. 1289, 1321 (E.D.Pa.1973), aff'd as to injunctive relief, Goode v. Rizzo, 506 F.2d 542 (3d Cir. 1974), cert. granted. But see Calvin v. Conlisk, 367 F.Supp. 476, 480 (N.D.Ill.1973).

**Legal approaches to judicially required rulemaking.**

The courts are quite capable of holding as a matter of common law that administrators are required to make rules. That is essentially what the Supreme Court did in the Ruiz case. But other techniques that are

## Ch. 6  *REQUIRED POLICE RULEMAKING*

available may be superior, including such judicial tools as (1) due process, (2) the nondelegation doctrine, and (3) the void for vagueness doctrine.

(1) The simplest and easiest approach may be the one the court used in Holmes v. New York City Housing Authority, 398 F.2d 262 (2d Cir. 1968): "Due process requires that selections among applicants be made in accordance with 'ascertainable standards.'" The question of which applicants get the housing, when the supply is insufficient for all applicants, may not be decided in the individual case except on the basis of ascertainable standards. That can be called a requirement of due process. In the same way, the question which persons are to be arrested for a given offense, when some are to be arrested and some not, may not be decided in the individual case except through ascertainable standards. A court can simply say that due process so requires, as the court did say in the Holmes case.

(2) An alternative approach, with the same results, is via the nondelegation doctrine. The courts have long interpreted constitutions (federal and state) to mean that legislative bodies may not delegate power without meaningful standards to guide the exercise of the power. But the legislative

bodies have not responded, and the nondelegation doctrine as developed by the courts has failed. The plain fact is that federal and state agencies *are* exercising vast delegated power without meaningful statutory standards. Outstanding cases involving great administrative power that is unguided by meaningful statutory standards include United States v. Southwestern Cable Co., 392 U.S. 157 (1968); American Trucking Ass'n v. Atchison, T. & S. F. Ry., 387 U.S. 397 (1967); Permian Basin Area Rate Cases, 390 U.S. 747 (1968).

The courts, I think, are right that meaningful standards are needed, especially when discretionary power is exercised in individual cases. Yet the Supreme Court in such cases as those just cited, as well as in many more, permits the exercise of discretionary power in individual cases without meaningful standards, because the legislative bodies have refused to provide the meaningful standards. That result seems to me somewhat unsatisfactory, and yet I see no prospect that the legislative bodies will be able and willing to provide the required standards. The way out is in my opinion what I proposed at page 58 of my 1969 book on Discretionary Justice: "I propose that the courts should continue their requirement of mean-

Ch. 6  *REQUIRED POLICE RULEMAKING*

ingful standards, except that when the legislative body fails to prescribe the required standards the administrators should be allowed to satisfy the requirement by prescribing them within a reasonable time."

The courts seem to me to be in process of adopting this idea. The only three Justices of the Supreme Court who have dealt with the idea in formal opinion have seemingly approved it, even reaching out for it in an opinion in which it was seemingly irrelevant. McGautha v. California, 402 U.S. 183, 273–74 (1971). The state courts seem to be adopting the idea. E. g., Barry & Barry v. Department of Motor Vehicles, 81 Wash.2d 155, 500 P.2d 540 (1972); People v. Fields, 391 Mich. 206, 216 N.W.2d 51 (1974); Sun Ray Drive-In Dairy v. Oregon Liquor Control Comm., 517 P.2d 289 (Ore.App.1973).

Even though the selective enforcement power of the police does not rest on an explicit delegation of power, the courts can hold that the constitutional requirement of meaningful standards is fully applicable. Indeed, the reasons for imposing that requirement in absence of explicit delegation are even stronger than they are when the power is explicitly delegated, for the need for judicial protection becomes stronger when administrative power grows up without statutory authorization. The less the legislative attention to what the administrators are doing, the greater the need for judicial attention.

(3) The third approach is in some ways the most desirable of the three in that it requires judicial analysis of the degree of injustice if courts do not require administrative rulemaking in particular circumstances. The best case for illustrative purposes, so far as I know, is Papachristou v. City of Jacksonville, 405 U.S. 156 (1972), holding a vagrancy ordinance unconstitutional. The decision rests on two reasons—lack of notice of what is permitted, and encouragement of arbitrary and discriminatory enforcement. Probably either reason can alone suffice for unconstitutionality, depending on the facts, and the one that is important to the present discussion is the second. The unanimous Court asserted: "Where, as here, there are no standards governing the exercise of discretion granted by the ordinance, the scheme permits and encourages arbitrary and discriminatory enforcement." I strongly agree. The ordinance must be held invalid because its vagueness permits and encourages arbitrary and discriminatory enforcement. The ordinance listed about 21 classes of "vagrants," including "rogues and vaga-

Ch. 6  *REQUIRED POLICE RULEMAKING*

bonds, . . . thieves, . . . persons wandering or strolling around from place to place without any lawful purpose or object . . ." The four who were arrested were not loafers; one was enrolled in a job-training program, one was a teacher, one was a full-time college student and a part-time computer helper, and one was a tow-motor operator in a grocery chain warehouse. The two white females and the two black males were in one car when they were arrested; the arresting officers denied that the racial mixture played any part in the decision to make the arrest.

The Court's statement that lack of guiding standards "permits and encourages arbitrary and discriminatory enforcement" seems to be fully supported. The ordinance is so vague that the arresting officers had hardly any guidance from it; they said they arrested the two men for having no identification and because the officers did not believe their story. The arbitrariness is shown in various ways, including this observation by the Court: "The codefendant was charged with 'loitering' because he was standing in the driveway, an act which the officers admitted was done only at their command."

A basic question that seems worth raising is this: What if a statute is clear, and the vagueness is in the enforcement policy? For instance, if the police enforce a clear statute against only ten out of a hundred known violators, and no one can know in advance which ten will be selected or why, is the system unconstitutional on the ground that, in the Court's words, it permits and encourages arbitrary and discriminatory enforcement of the law? My answer is that the vagueness of the enforcement policy is at least as important as the vagueness of a statute or ordinance, for it just as much permits and encourages arbitrary and discriminatory enforcement of the law. Indeed, vagueness of enforcement policy is worse than vagueness of legislation, because vagueness of legislation can be cured by a clear and open enforcement policy, but not the other way around.

The Court quite properly responded to the problem before it in asserting that lack of standards in the ordinance is unconstitutional. But I think the fundamental may be broader—that vagueness of law or of enforcement policy is unconstitutional because it permits or encourages arbitrary and discriminatory enforcement of the law. Although I do not predict immediate judicial adoption of that fundamental, because the tasks of working out the limits and applica-

## Ch. 6 REQUIRED POLICE RULEMAKING

tions are enormous and because more widespread thinking about the problem may well be a prerequisite, I do predict that the time will come when courts will generally hold that unnecessary or undue vagueness in an enforcement policy is unconstitutional, because of the reasons the unanimous Supreme Court stated in the Papachristou opinion.

Neither legislatures nor courts can or should determine the details of enforcement policies, but either legislatures or courts can and should require that enforcement policies be clarified through administrative rulemaking. Accordingly, courts should as rapidly as feasible move toward requiring the police to correct both the vagueness and the concealment of the enforcement policy.

Although I do not disagree either with the Papachristou holding or with any part of the opinion, I think that in the future vague statutes can be sustained on condition that administrators through rulemaking provide the needed clarification. The basic legal rule should be that police who are enforcing vague legislation have the responsibility to formulate open rules that will sufficiently correct the vagueness. Since vagueness of legislation may be a denial of due process, courts in the name of due process may require rulemaking.

# CHAPTER 7

# THE RIGHT MIX OF RULE AND DISCRETION

**The present mix.**

Chicago patrolmen have far too much discretionary power. They should not have to resolve questions of overall policy in individual cases; high officers should resolve such questions through rulemaking. Discretion of patrolmen should be limited to what is required for individualizing.

Although exercise of discretion is the essence of police work and is indispensable, and although rulemaking can stifle effectiveness if it goes too far, discretion in the Chicago police department must be drastically cut back. Far more rulemaking is needed.

The main goal should be to achieve the right mix of rule and discretion. The present mix is wrong. A better balance can easily be created. Unnecessary discretion should be eliminated, and necessary discretion should be properly confined, properly structured, and properly checked.

The subject of rule and discretion is confusing to those who have not carefully stud-

Ch. 7 *MIX OF RULE AND DISCRETION*

ied it, and even the most perceptive officers, including those at high levels, fall into the same common misunderstandings about it. In our interviews, officers at all levels have almost always assumed that making a rule on a subject eliminates discretion on that subject; they properly perceive that discretion is essential, and then they improperly assume that a rule would necessarily be harmful. What they do not readily see is that *a particular subject may call for a rule that does not cut into needed discretion.*

Because such misunderstandings are so common, and because they can be corrected with some plodding analysis, the rest of this chapter will be devoted to some rather elementary observations about rule and discretion.

### Should police discretion be eliminated?

Police discretion is absolutely essential. It cannot be eliminated. Any effort to eliminate it would be ridiculous. Discretion is the essence of police work, both in law enforcement and in service activities. Police work without discretion would be something like a human torso without legs, arms, or head.

That police discretion cannot be eliminated is an eternal and unalterable proposition.

But that proposition is entirely consistent with two other essential propositions—that excessive or unnecessary discretion can and should be eliminated, and that necessary discretion should be properly controlled.

For instance, an Illinois statute makes gambling a crime, with a special exception for bingo in some circumstances, but without a general exception for social gambling. The Chicago police have been quite clear that anyone who engages in gambling that involves a commercial element should be arrested, but they have been somewhat unclear about social gambling, such as a poker game at the home of one of the players. We have asked this question of a good many officers: "If a wife complains to you that her husband is in an all-night poker game at an address she gives, and she asks you to break up the game and to arrest the gamblers, what do you do?" We got three answers: (1) We arrest the players. (2) We break up the game but we do not usually arrest. (3) We tell her that we don't enforce against social gamblers. People in the gambling section of the vice control division say that they do not deal with this type of question and that the policy is made wholly in the 21 police districts. The department

## Ch. 7  MIX OF RULE AND DISCRETION

clearly has no policy. Patrolmen are free to do as they choose.

I think a rule on social gambling is clearly desirable. A decision about the substance of the rule should depend upon what comes out of a rulemaking proceeding. But I would suggest a proposed rule along this line: "In absence of special circumstances, we do not ordinarily arrest for social gambling in absence of (a) a complaint, (b) a profit from the gambling other than gambling winnings, or (c) extraordinarily high stakes. When we receive a complaint, we ordinarily investigate, but for first offenders we may break up social gambling without making arrests." Perhaps a rule could define the meaning of "extraordinarily high stakes."

Such a rule will not eliminate needed discretion but, like a magnet, will pull the diversity of opinion among officers toward a more uniform policy, and I think that will be desirable. The rule will pull toward equal justice, without cutting into needed discretion. Such words as "in the absence of special circumstances" and "ordinarily" leave room for discretion, and they probably leave enough room for discretion. Such words, of course, can be adjusted to enlarge or to restrict the discretion.

The main point of my gambling illustration does not have to do with gambling but has to do with the right mix of rule and discretion. The main point is that *a rule may reduce unnecessary discretion without cutting into needed discretion.* That observation applies not merely to a rule on gambling but also to hundreds of problems of enforcement the department now leaves to the discretion of patrolmen.

### Why unnecessary discretion is undesirable.

Since discretion of police and of other administrative officers is absolutely essential, why not just resolve all questions about rule and discretion in favor of allowing unlimited and unguided discretion? Doesn't the officer on the spot, who knows all the immediate facts and circumstances, have a better basis for a wise decision than any rule writers can have?

The reason for limiting and guiding discretion is *not* that human beings cannot exercise unlimited and unguided discretion wisely, justly, and beneficently. They often can. They often do. The reason is that out of a thousand officers, no matter how well screened, a large portion may be expected to abuse their power to a considerable extent, and some—perhaps only a few—are likely to

Ch. 7  *MIX OF RULE AND DISCRETION*

engage in occasional abuse of power that is quite serious. This statement about the basic nature of the human being is not controversial. Thoughtful people readily confirm it from their own observation and experience. Of course, everyone who lives among people has a foundation for making his own determination.

Even though my own subjective belief is that a good many federal judges I have known have unblemished integrity and thoroughly sound judgment and can therefore safely be trusted with a good deal of unguided discretionary power, still I think the framers of our constitutional and legal systems have been wise to invent many ways to confine, structure, and check the discretionary power of federal judges, because human weaknesses and inadequacies are readily perceptible in *some* federal judges.

We need not reach the question whether the reasons for limiting and guiding the discretion of the Chicago police are greater than they are for federal judges. The reasons, I believe, are at least as strong, and that is enough. This conclusion is perfectly consistent with the observation that *some* members of the Chicago police force may have such integrity and judgment that they could safely be trusted with unlimited and unguided discretionary power.

## Why confining, structuring, and checking of necessary discretion is desirable.

The reasons just given for trying to eliminate unnecessary discretion also support the idea that necessary discretion should be confined, structured, and checked.

A rule that confines discretion says to the officer: "Here are the boundaries of your discretion. You are free to make your own choices within this area, but don't go outside the boundaries." A rule that structures discretion says to the officer: "Within the area in which you have discretionary power, let your discretion be guided by these goals, policies, and principles, and follow these procedures that are designed to minimize arbitrariness." Discretion of an officer is "checked" when it is reviewed by a supervisor, by a prosecutor, by a judge, by a private party, by the press, by legislators, or by someone else; discretion that is checked is obviously less likely to be arbitrary than discretion that is unchecked.

In working out their law enforcement policies, Chicago patrolmen often exercise unconfined, unstructured, and unchecked discretionary power. For instance, their dis-

## Ch. 7  *MIX OF RULE AND DISCRETION*

cretion to arrest for disorderly conduct is almost entirely unconfined. Mild words which accurately assert that the officer is abusing his authority are subject to punishment by arrest, even if the officer knows that the arrest is false, and even if the officer has no intent to give testimony in court that the conduct was disorderly. Many officers have freely acknowledged to us that they often make such arrests that they know they could not support with testimony. A rule could provide that words alone, other than fighting words, can never justify an arrest.

Our interviews show that the Chicago police are normally very sensitive to verbal defiance. One who manifests antagonism to the officer may be arrested for disorderly conduct, and to make the arrest the officer may have to resort to force. Out of such a setting grows a good deal of the alleged police brutality. I am surprised that the Chicago police have no rules on the subject; they should have. What is most needed is nothing more than a simple rule that will capture the heart of what the Supreme Court has often unanimously held—that verbal defiance, without fighting words, does not justify either an arrest or a resort to force. A clear rule, if the supervisors could get it not only into the book but also into the consciousness of each patrolman, could be more beneficial than all the work of all the review boards, which, after all, operate on problems only after the harm has been done. Surely the police should at least experiment with such a rule.

Even when a rule to *govern* the officer's behavior is undesirable because the nature of the subject matter requires a good deal of individualizing, a set of rules to *structure or guide* the officer's discretion may be helpful. For instance, almost every officer in the Chicago police department assumes that a set of rules on what an officer should do in handling a serious fight between spouses could not possibly be helpful or satisfactory, because an officer has to feel his way along and cannot follow rules. But my opinion is that *guiding* rules even on such subject matter may be helpful and can be written in such a way that they will never be harmful. For instance, guiding rules may provide that the officer may properly try to separate the parties, should usually try to take weapons away from them, should listen to both disputants before taking a position on issues of fact, should try to give an appearance of impartiality in ruling on issues of fact, should try to reduce tension, should strive to limit police intervention as much as is consistent

Ch. 7  *MIX OF RULE AND DISCRETION*

with main objectives of restoring peace, should normally refrain from physically restraining either party until mediation and warnings have failed, and usually should make arrests only as a last resort. Rules which do nothing more than make mild suggestions about general objectives and goals in dealing with specified problems can greatly improve police effectiveness and enhance the quality of police justice. *The Chicago police need far more such guiding rules.*

Checking is one of the best ways to prevent or correct abuse of discretion. When a patrolman arrests for a petty offense, a sergeant or lieutenant may inquire: "Why did you waste your time on that?" That kind of gentle checking may be quite effective. But not enough is done, perhaps, to check the failure to make arrests that ought to be made. When an officer gets a radio direction to investigate, he has to report what he finds, but when an officer makes an investigation on his own initiative, the checking is less than it would be if required reporting were firmly enforced. And the checking of illegal harassment is very slight—much less than it might be. Superior officers who verbally disapprove particular kinds of harassment in our interviews usually acknowledge that they do little or nothing to discourage or to prevent it.

**Rules do not necessarily replace discretion.**

The usual unthinking assumption is that an officer either follows a rule or exercises discretion. The assumption is seldom in accord with reality. I insist that rule and discretion are not always mutually exclusive, and in so insisting I am not quibbling but trying to emphasize the highly practical fact that rules often overlap with discretion. A rule may provide that the officer must not decide except through exercise of discretion based on the answers to six designated questions of fact. Such a rule does not replace discretion but it requires the exercise of discretion, and it guides the discretion by requiring answers to the six questions. Rules which require the exercise of discretion are exceedingly important; rules on what to do and what not to do with a hostile, riotous crowd may be mainly of that character. If all rules were designed to replace discretion, about half the value of rules would be gone.

Some rules replace discretion; some rules do not. Some rules limit discretion beyond a designated point but provide for discretion up to that point. Some rules reinforce discre-

## Ch. 7  MIX OF RULE AND DISCRETION

tion. Many, many rules guide discretion, including some of the most useful rules.

A single set of rules may to some extent provide for discretion, to some extent reinforce discretion, to some extent limit discretion, to some extent replace discretion, and to some extent guide discretion.

Rules may be written or unwritten. In the Chicago police department, the written rules—those of the Police Board, the general orders, and the special orders—contain almost nothing about enforcement policy. But the ordinary patrolman often is significantly guided on enforcement policy by the unwritten rules he has picked up from his colleagues and his superiors. Indeed, some unwritten rules seem to be based on misinformation or myth, and yet such rules may be followed with remarkable unanimity.

Some rules are in the nature of a habit. A patrolman says: "My rule is to give the boy a fatherly talk, perhaps scare him a bit, and let him go." That may be a "rule," even though discretion is not cut off; the same patrolman may be inspired to adapt his "rule" to special circumstances; that is, he may modify the rule, thereby reasserting discretion. A rule may be a set of precedents. Just as lawyers say that "the

[*150*]

*MIX OF RULE AND DISCRETION* Ch. 7

common law rule is so and so," the police may say, on the basis of two or three incidents, that "our rule is to do this."

A rule may be precise and rigid, it may be broad and vague, or it may be anything between. In lawyers' language, a rule may be only a standard, that is, a very vague statement. A vague standard may be consistent with a degree of discretion that is almost one hundred percent. The Illinois Juvenile Court Act, which guides youth officers, requires "a spirit of humane concern"; that is a vague standard and it is also a rule.

**Choosing the mix of rule and discretion.**

Most practical problems about rule and discretion do not involve choosing between rule and discretion; they involve choosing between one mix of rule and discretion and another mix of rule and discretion. Discretion is seldom zero and seldom one hundred percent; it is almost always well above zero and well below a hundred.

For instance, a patrolman encounters a 16-year-old boy smoking marijuana in a public place. What should the officer do? The answer cannot possibly be so fully covered by rules that the officer's discretion will be zero in all circumstances, for imaginations of rule writers are inadequate to accomplish that result. The boy might be dying, he might be looking at a gun pointed at his head, he might be selling heroin to teenagers, he might be one of a crowd who are so hostile to the officer as to make arrest impossible, and he might be part of an elaborate trap set for the officer; rules cannot possibly reach all of the real life that is stranger than fiction.

Similarly, making the discretion absolute is almost impossible. Discretion is almost never one hundred percent. Even if the only fact the officer knows is that the boy is smoking marijuana and the only question he tries to answer is whether to make an arrest, his discretion is much less than one hundred per cent, even though he is subject to no order from any superior, in the form of a rule or otherwise, either to arrest or not to arrest.

Even for this exceedingly simple problem, the Chicago patrolman is in fact subject to a mix of rule and discretion with at least eight main ingredients:

(1) The Illinois statute makes possession of marijuana a crime no matter how small the quantity. Most officers, high and low, assert that the statute leaves them no discretionary power to decide not to make the

arrest. That view may seem to be attractive theory, but it is obviously contrary to the realities. (2) The formal rules and regulations of the Chicago Police Board, printed and published and widely distributed, provide penalties against officers who fail to "enforce all laws and ordinances." Every patrolman every day fails to "enforce all laws and ordinances" and violates the formal rules and regulations. (3) The dominant attitude of supervising officers—sergeants, lieutenants, watch commanders, and district commanders—is that the arrest should ordinarily be made. Yet many of them are not at all informed about patrolmen's practices, and many of them know nothing of prosecutors' and judges' practices. (4) The supervising officers generally issue no orders and make no suggestions to patrolmen on the subject. (5) No general order and no special order from the superintendent deals with the question. The general orders and special orders hardly touch problems of law enforcement policy, such as this one. (6) Youth officers generally release a 16-year-old whose only offense is smoking marijuana, but the question infrequently comes up, because patrolmen seldom take the juvenile into custody for such an offense. When patrolmen learn that youth officers release the

## Ch. 7 MIX OF RULE AND DISCRETION

juvenile, their practice about taking juveniles into custody is of course influenced. (7) Almost all patrolmen say they believe a prosecutor will not prosecute and a court will not convict for merely smoking marijuana. Whether they are right or wrong in this, their belief is in fact *the* most important factor that determines the prevailing policy of the Chicago police on the subject. The policy is made by patrolmen, and it is not made on the basis of a consideration of the merits of the question whether or not an arrest is desirable. Nor is it based on what the statute provides. (8) The second most important influence on any particular patrolman is likely to be his knowledge that his colleagues generally do not make the arrest.

The eight factors add up to something much less than absolute discretion. A superficial look at the question of arresting or not arresting for smoking marijuana would lead to a quick conclusion that the officer has complete discretion. A closer look shows that his discretion is affected by the confused complex of eight factors. And the example we are discussing is more or less typical of enforcement policies of the Chicago police.

The main point I am trying to make is that on a scale from zero to a hundred, discretion is almost always well above zero and almost always well below a hundred. Practical choices are not between rule and discretion; they are between one mix of rule and discretion and a different mix of rule and discretion. What officers tend to assume to be a choice between rule and discretion may turn out on closer examination to be a choice between, say, forty and sixty on the scale.

On many, many subjects the Chicago police need to reduce discretion from something like sixty on the scale to something like forty. That kind of movement will not eliminate discretion and it will seldom eliminate discretion on any particular subject.

What is needed is the right mix of rule and discretion.

Now, while we have the eight factors in mind, let us consider some other aspects. Would good management of the department subject the patrolman to influences pulling in both directions on such a simple question as whether or not to arrest for smoking marijuana? The losses from the conflicting and confusing influences are probably not very great on that one subject. But what are the losses from a thousand or ten thousand such subjects? If this subject is typi-

## Ch. 7 *MIX OF RULE AND DISCRETION*

cal, as I think it is more or less, is the efficiency of the total operation vitally impaired? Could the 13,400 officers accomplish twice as much if the confusing complex were replaced by a clear and simple rule? Or could the same job be done by half as many?

Of course, if we think of the marijuana problem as a sample of hundreds of somewhat comparable problems, as we should, we can quickly see that the failure is much broader than that of the managers of the department. Part of the failure is that of the legislative bodies for including much too much in criminal legislation; in this instance, the statute is unrealistic in making possession of a tiny quantity of marijuana a crime, as is proved by the refusal of officers to arrest, the refusal of prosecutors to prosecute, and the refusal of courts to convict. Part of the failure is also that of the police board, whose formal rules and regulations defeat their own basic purpose. Telling police officers that they will be penalized if they do not "enforce all laws and ordinances" is an absurdity unless the legislative bodies modify a good many statutes and ordinances. Part of the failure also lies in the absence of legal advisers. The many supervising officers who have asserted to us in our interviews that the arrest should be made probably should have access to legal advice about what prosecutors and judges do. And the same remark may be made about many other subjects.

The main failure on the marijuana problem is surely that of the superintendent. The department should have some sort of rule on the subject instead of leaving patrolmen free to do whatever they choose in each case. A simple rule could provide that in absence of special circumstances, an arrest ordinarily should not be made when the only offense is smoking marijuana and possession of not more than —— grams of marijuana. Such a rule would largely correct all the other failures. Although the rule would accomplish very little on the question of arresting or not arresting the smoker, since the present practices of nearly all patrolmen are uniform on that question, the proposed rule would bring the few dissenting patrolmen into line and would accomplish a good deal by fixing the minimum for which an arrest should ordinarily be made. Amending the statute to prescribe a minimum would be preferable, but the problem I am discussing is what the police should do in absence of such an amendment. The best solution would be a statutory amendment. The next

Ch. 7  *MIX OF RULE AND DISCRETION*

best would be a police rule. The worst solution is the present one—neither an amendment nor a rule but a confusing complex of eight factors, along with a vast variety of practices about the minimum amount.

The main thrust of my remarks does not have to do with marijuana but with the police system of taking care of such problems —or not taking care of them. On hundreds of subjects, the department should provide patrolmen with rules that govern or rules that guide.

### General policy calls for rules; individualizing calls for discretion.

The main principle that should guide the choice of the mix of rule and discretion can be simply stated: The more general the question of policy the greater the rule content of the mix; the more the need for individualizing the greater the discretion content of the mix.

The Chicago police depart from that sound principle in leaving overall enforcement policy for patrolmen to decide in individual cases. Sometimes patrolmen do exceedingly well in developing reasonably uniform enforcement policies, but sometimes they do not.

## MIX OF RULE AND DISCRETION  Ch. 7

A Chicago ordinance makes it a crime to drink an alcoholic beverage in a park. A patrolman encounters a family picnic. The man and woman are openly drinking beer with their meal. The family is well behaved and quiet, except for normal laughter and cries of the children. Should the patrolman interfere? Should he arrest? Should he ask the family to put the beer away and to drink no more of it? Should he seize the beer and pour it out on the grass? Or should he smile, say a cheering word, and walk on? Should a rule guide the officer? What should be the mix of rule and discretion?

I think the answers are not difficult. The ordinance, taken literally, obviously overshoots. Those who adopted it probably did not mean to prohibit beer or wine at an orderly family picnic; they probably meant to reach drunkenness, disorder, and disturbing the enjoyment of others. The ordinance is typical of the tendency of legislative bodies to prohibit too much, relying on administrators to adopt sensible enforcement policies which will produce reasonable results. On the basis of that interpretation of the ordinance, the police, in my opinion, might well adopt a rule that they do not ordinarily enforce the ordinance in absence of drunken-

## Ch. 7  MIX OF RULE AND DISCRETION

ness, noise, or disturbance of others, but they may take into account a violation of the ordinance in deciding a close question of whether or not to arrest for another reason. Such a rule would pull together the occasional disparate results, but it would not change the mainstream results of the present system.

A rule on the subject seems to me to be needed, even though most patrolmen in the illustrative case would refuse to make an arrest. For a good system, even a complete uniformity of nonarrest is not enough; those affected must have a chance to know what the enforcement policy is, and they only sometimes have that chance now. Some of the 21 district offices we telephoned anonymously said, mostly falsely, that we would be arrested if we drank in the park on a family picnic. That answer can be harmful to an inquirer, and it is inexcusable. A rule could and should prevent that answer. Of course, my remarks are not limited to drinking in the park; that is only one illustration of what I think the function of police rules should be.

The rule I propose sets forth the general policy, while at the same time leaving plenty of discretionary leeway for the officer to do whatever individualizing he deems necessary. The rule should not be so rigid and precise as to exclude discretion. The word "ordinarily" is a good one that leaves room for discretion. The words "drunkenness," "noise," and "disturbance" all have some degree of imprecision, leaving appropriate room for discretion. I think my rule produces about the right mix of rule and discretion, but it can be adjusted to whatever degree is deemed desirable.

My proposed rule can do much good in some circumstances. It would counteract the unfortunate tendency of some patrolmen to think in the way the police board thinks when it solemnly asserts that officers must "enforce all laws and ordinances." Most officers know that they should not enforce all laws and ordinances, but they should not be told that they must. My proposed rule would bolster the sound reaction of the sensible patrolman who knows that interrupting the family picnic would accomplish nothing. It would also pull away from, but would not fully protect against, an abuse of power by wrongly invoking the ordinance, as would happen, for instance, if the patrolman would invoke the ordinance against drinking in the park as a means of ousting a black family from a part of the park that is by custom reserved for whites. Of course, the very

## Ch. 7  MIX OF RULE AND DISCRETION

subject of making delicate adjustments on various problems of race relations is itself a subject that calls for rulemaking—the right mix of rule and discretion.

Among the hundreds of subjects on which rulemaking by the Chicago police is especially needed, some may call for little or no room for individualizing. An example is the problem of what a patrolman should do when the victim of a crime is unwilling to sign a complaint. This problem especially calls for rulemaking because (a) policy ideas differ widely within the department, (b) some policies may be based on misimpressions of policies of prosecutors and judges, and (c) preferences of the public may differ from what the police assume them to be. Rules might generally govern the answers to such questions as these: When one boy steals another boy's bicycle, should the officer release the thief if the owner so requests, or should the thief always be taken into custody and turned over to a youth officer? If a policeman catches a woman in the act of shoplifting, should the officer himself sign the complaint, out of respect for the interests of other merchants, even if the particular merchant refuses to sign it? If the victim of armed robbery is so intimidated by the robber that he asks the officer to release him on the spot, should the officer for the safety of that victim release the robber, or should the officer for the protection of future victims of that robber insist on arresting him? Such questions as these, I think, should be answered not only through rules but also through rulemaking procedure, for the views of legislators, judges, and prosecutors should be sought, as well as views of members of the public. Of course, one of the questions that should be worked out through the rulemaking procedure is the extent to which room should be left for individualizing.

# CHAPTER 8

# SUMMARY AND CONCLUSIONS

Some law the Chicago police always or almost always enforce, some law they never or almost never enforce, and some law they enforce if, as, and when they choose. They select not only the law they enforce but also the persons and the occasions. Their discretion to enforce or not to enforce is enormous and is seldom limited or guided by rules or instructions. The focus of this essay is discretionary selective enforcement.

Twenty samples of nonenforcement of criminal statutes and ordinances are listed in the second section of chapter 1. Most of them relate to minor crimes but some involve felonies. The rest of that chapter shows the difficulty and complexity of some problems of enforcement policy. For instance, the section on prostitution identifies ten particular questions of mixed policy and fact that seem to me to call for answers through investigations, studies, and give and take among those interested.

Enforcement policy is not based on studies, and specialized professional staffs do not contribute to it. It is made primarily by patrolmen, the least qualified in the organization of 13,400, and they do not even have access to legal advisers. Their policy often varies widely from one officer to another, and it characteristically rests on offhand and quick judgments. Patrolmen can do very little toward coordinating the policy they make with the policy of prosecutors and judges. These gross deficiencies in the making of policy are the subject of chapter 2.

Such deficiencies stem directly from the pervasive false pretense of full enforcement, to which chapter 3 is devoted. Officers at all levels know that the system is one of selective enforcement, but they have an elaborate system of pretending that all statutes and ordinances are fully enforced. Superiors never instruct subordinates to refrain in any circumstances from enforcing any law. No general order or special order calls for nonenforcement. General order 70–4 provides: "The district watch commander will . . . direct the enforcement of all laws and ordinances and the rules, regulations, and orders of the Department . . ." It contains no exception to the words "all laws and ordinances." The Chicago police board in its published rules and regulations, which are supposed to govern the department, for-

## Ch. 8 SUMMARY AND CONCLUSIONS

mally asserts without qualification that all officers have a duty to "enforce all laws and ordinances."

The combination of selective enforcement with a comprehensive pretense of full enforcement is deeply established. It is the only system the present personnel have ever known, the system on which they were brought up when they first began their police work, the system the department has followed for more than a century, the system that is apparently followed by all American police departments.

The reason for that system is quite clear: The police are caught between their belief that they are required to enforce fully and their lack of sufficient resources for full enforcement. They fail to enforce fully and, in human fashion, they try to hide their failure. At the same time they privately insist that full enforcement is both impossible and undesirable. I fully agree. Indeed, I regard their recognition of the need for selective enforcement as a significant accomplishment, which is all the greater in that the barrier of their supposed obligation to enforce fully has had to be overcome.

The false pretense seems to me unfortunate, not merely because truth is better than falsity, but because many harms flow from the falsity: It prevents high officers from making enforcement policy, it prevents studies by specialized professional staffs to determine what enforcement policies are desirable, and it prevents open planning for coordination of police enforcement policies with the policies of prosecutors and judges. Because the false pretense is extremely harmful, I think it should be replaced by an honest system of open selective enforcement, which in my opinion will be entirely legal. The superintendent and the five deputy superintendents seem surprised by my legal opinion, for it is the opposite of what they and their predecessors have assumed for more than a century, but some of them have acknowledged that they have never sought legal advice on the question and that they know of no instance when their predecessors have. My legal analysis is set forth in chapter 4. I do not deny that the full enforcement legislation is clear and unambiguous, but I find that legislative intent elsewhere expressed is stronger, including longterm legislative reliance on police and prosecutors to cut back criminal legislation known to the legislators to be excessive, and including the appropriation of enough for only an estimat-. ed one-half to two-thirds of full enforcement.

## Ch. 8 SUMMARY AND CONCLUSIONS

My thesis is not only that selective enforcement should be open and aboveboard but also that enforcement policy should be made through the kind of rulemaking procedure that has been highly successful in federal administrative agencies, a procedure that, so far as I know, American police have never used. Rulemaking procedure is fully discussed in chapter 5. The police should prepare proposed rules on the basis of staff studies, publish them, invite written comments from any member of the public, revise on the basis of the comments, and then publish the final rules. They should freely amend the rules from time to time to keep up with developing understanding and changing conditions. Especially important to my main thesis is the final section of chapter 5, stating and explaining fourteen reasons in favor of police rulemaking on selective enforcement. My own opinion is that those reasons are overwhelming.

The police should voluntarily move to a system of rulemaking, but if they do not, I think the time will come when the courts will require them to make rules. Chapter 6 presents the new judicial case law that has rapidly developed during the past few years on judicially required administrative rulemaking. Three cases already require police

[168]

rulemaking, but not yet on the subject of selective enforcement. Various judicial techniques for imposing that requirement are discussed in chapter 6.

One potential technique, still unrealized, can have momentous results and deserves thoughtful consideration. The Supreme Court of the United States has held an ordinance unconstitutional on the ground that its vagueness "permits and encourages arbitrary and discriminatory enforcement of the law." The vagueness was in the ordinance. What if the ordinance had been clear, but it was enforced in only one-tenth of the cases to which its words apply, and no one affected could know in advance which cases would be chosen or on what basis? Could vagueness of an enforcement policy make it unconstitutional on the ground that it "permits and encourages arbitrary and discriminatory enforcement of the law"? I think the courts will and should move gradually to an affirmative answer. Perhaps all of us who work on legal problems should be wondering whether judicial opinions, lawyers' thinking, and legal education are too much focused on the formality of law (words in statutes and in case law) and give insufficient emphasis to the reality of law (what enforcement officers do in fact).

## Ch. 8  SUMMARY AND CONCLUSIONS

Chapter 7, entitled The Right Mix of Rule and Discretion, deals in somewhat elementary fashion with a vital subject that deserves far more attention than it has had. The present mix in the Chicago police department is wrong. More rules are needed. Discretion must be cut back. Unnecessary discretion must be eliminated. But discretion often is necessary and often must be preserved. Necessary discretion must be properly confined, structured, and checked.

The superintendent and the five deputy superintendents initially reject the idea that they need more rules. Each of them engages in the same three-step reasoning: (1) Police discretion is essential. (2) Rules would necessarily replace discretion. (3) Therefore rules would be harmful. I think their first step is entirely right, but the conclusion is unsound because the second step involves a clear misunderstanding. Rules need not replace discretion. My opinion is that when the Chicago police begin to experiment with rulemaking on enforcement policy they will discover for themselves this basic principle: Rules may limit and may guide discretion without cutting into needed discretion, and such rules may be exceedingly useful.

## SUMMARY AND CONCLUSIONS  Ch. 8

The practical choice is hardly ever between rule and discretion. It is almost always between one mix of rule and discretion and another mix. For example, on a scale on which discretion is from zero to one hundred percent, the choice is almost never between a hundred and zero, and it is seldom between twenty or less and eighty or more. The need may often be for a change from something like sixty to something like forty, and such a change may be from the wrong mix to the right mix.

The principal goal with respect to the mix of rule and discretion in a police department is easy to state: A patrolman should not have discretion about overall enforcement policy but should have discretion to do the needed individualizing in applying the policy made by his superiors to the facts and circumstances of each particular case. When discretion is needed for individualizing, rules should properly limit it and should properly guide it, but should not replace it.

\*

# APPENDIX

## The Why and the How of this Study

This is a sequel to my 1969 book entitled Discretionary Justice—A Preliminary Inquiry, in which I attempted to open the way into the neglected subject of what to do about uncontrolled discretion of governmental administrators. The preparation of that book brought me to the realization of two new ideas—that the eighty or ninety percent of the administrative process involving informal and unreviewed discretionary action has been neglected even though that part of the administrative process is where most of the injustice is located, and that administrative law thinking has never been applied to police or prosecutors but should be. The present project tries to develop those two ideas as they apply to the police.

This study began with my reading of police literature. My broad purpose was to identify the discretionary powers of the police and to find out how and to what extent they are controlled. I soon found that the largest cluster of discretionary action pertains to selective enforcement, and my in-

## APPENDIX

quiry began to focus on that subject. But the literature bearing on selective enforcement is insufficient, although some particular items are excellent, and I could go no further except by interviewing.

During the spring of 1974, with funds from the Ford Foundation, I employed five research assistants for full-time interviewing in the Chicago police department from June 15 to September 15, and I sent a letter on April 19 to Superintendent James M. Rochford, requesting permission to interview. But he gave me only equivocal and delaying answers, and I found that tight controls prevented our interviewing without formal permission. By letter of June 20, I made clear that we would not inquire into corruption, brutality, or racial discrimination, and that we would not interview any officer except at his convenience and with his full consent and cooperation. Even after my assistants had been on the payroll for two weeks, we still awaited permission to do the interviewing.

When the authorization finally came on July 2, it was coupled with a restriction that a representative of the department's division of research and development must be present at each interview, because "Some members of the department may be unrelia-

*APPENDIX*

ble and we want to protect your study from untrue facts about the department." The extra person sometimes listened but often seemed not to. Whether his presence restricted what would otherwise have been said we do not know. Yet we were repeatedly startled that so much was volunteered that was unfavorable to the department.

We interviewed about 300 officers, but counting them is difficult; when we talked with two men in a patrol car, along with the extra man, and the articulate one was dominant but the others made some remarks, how many were we interviewing? Even when our counting is precise, I usually prefer to say "about three-quarters" instead of 72 percent, because the analysis at no point depends on numerical exactness. After all, we interviewed only 300 out of 13,400. Our purpose is not to make scientific findings but to locate the general nature of practices and procedures, in order to work on the problems thus uncovered.

All the writing has been done by me, and I had a draft completed when I interviewed each of the five deputy superintendents and finally the superintendent. I spent a profitable two or three hours with each of them, and we talked much more about ideas than about facts. Yet I did not succeed in think-

*APPENDIX*

ing significantly with any one of them about ways to improve the thesis; they could hardly be expected to absorb it so quickly. My hope was to get their studied reactions to the manuscript. I revised it to reflect the interviews with them and sent a copy to each with a letter inviting criticisms. The only response was an unhelpful letter from the superintendent. Because no words of mine could transmit his attitude as effectively as his own words can, I asked his permission to publish his letter. He replied by letter that it was "a personal communication and not intended for publication."

So this study lacks two items that might have strengthened it—correction by the high officers of possible errors in the detailed facts, and their deliberated response to the ideas. But whatever the errors in details that might have been corrected, they are unlikely to affect the thesis, for it rests on the broad outline of facts that has been fully confirmed by the top officers.